WESTFALL CEMETERY

CEMETERY LAYOUT

Copley Township
Knox County
Illinois

Volume I

Michael T. Osler

HERITAGE BOOKS
2009

HERITAGE BOOKS

AN IMPRINT OF HERITAGE BOOKS, INC.

Books, CDs, and more—Worldwide

For our listing of thousands of titles see our website
at
www.HeritageBooks.com

Published 2009 by
HERITAGE BOOKS, INC.
Publishing Division
100 Railroad Ave. #104
Westminster, Maryland 21157

Other books by the author:

Westfall Cemetery, Copley Township, Knox County, Illinois: Cemetery History; Volume II

International Standard Book Numbers
Paperbound: 978-0-7884-5003-7
Clothbound: 978-0-7884-8192-5

For the Westfall family

This book is dedicated to my late Aunt, Joyce Westfall Taylor, who obtained the original plot records that started me on this path and my Great Aunt Ina White Westfall, who's decades of Westfall family research has contributed so much to this work. I also want to thank all of my Westfall relatives who have helped to make this possible.

In addition, a special appreciation goes to the Galesburg Register Mail, for allowing the use of their obituary information for this effort.

M.T. Osler

TABLE OF CONTENTS

PREFACE

The following pages contain a comprehensive look at the people who lived in and around that section of Copley Township that contains the Westfall Cemetery. It does this by analyzing their obituaries, reviewing the Census Records and attempting to determine how each family line is linked together.

The Cemetery was created by the Trusties of the Maxey Chapel, Methodist Episcopal Church. At that time, the trusties were relatives of the Westfall Family that lived near by. The Cemetery stayed in the care of the Westfall family for many years and then eventually was turned over to the county.

This project set out to establish the evidence to support a family understanding that everyone in the Cemetery was related to the Westfall family. To that end, with a few minor exceptions, I believe that I have accomplished this task.

Because of the large volume of data this information is being presented in two Volumes. Volume I contains the Cemetery Location and Plot Layout information along with special notes and observations from the actual sexton records. Volume II contains the 383 obituaries that have been gathered in this effort, along with other key source information to fill in the gaps where there is no obituary. Going forward there will be a Volume III that will contain all of the family trees and the connection of those trees to the Westfall family.

VIII

INTRODUCTION

HISTORY OF WESTFALL CEMETERY

Westfall Cemetery is located in the Southeast corner of the North West Quarter of Section twenty-nine (29), Copley Twp., Knox County, Illinois. The plot of land was purchased March 3, 1858 A.D. from Isaac E. Hurr of the county of Knox, state of Illinois by church trustees of the Methodist Episcopal Church. The trustees were Lewis Mitchell, Sylvanus Westfall, Lorenzo Lane, James Johnson and Gustavus Waddle. Purchase price for the three-acre plot was $24.00 of lawful money in hand. Deed of sale was recorded May 2, 1864 A.D. 2:00 P.M. at the Recorder of Deeds office, Knox County Court House, Galesburg, Illinois. The Deed states that the trustees and their successors shall build or cause to be erected a house or place of worship for the use of the members of the Methodist Episcopal Church in the United States of America.

The cemetery, located on the west two acres of the tract of land purchased by the church trustees, was named after the Westfall family. Alexander Westfall was buried here on Dec 17, 1862 at the age of 78 yrs. 8mos. 22days. All of the Westfall family lines buried here are descendants of Alexander. Alexander was among the earliest burials but according to record, was not the first.

It has been told that the families of the area cleared the cemetery from hazel brush making a total of 108 lots. One acre in front of cemetery of Oak trees next to the road was where the house of worship was to be located. Up keep of the cemetery in early days was done by each of the different families and small donations of money.

The original plot of three acres was surveyed by C. S. Richey, County Surveyor on Oct 30, 1894. In 1904, according to a newspaper article, the Cemetery was incorporated to be known as the Westfall Cemetery Association. The meeting was held at the home of Arthur Westergreen. Samuel Aston Westfall was elected sexton of the cemetery. Arthur Westergreen served as Secretary-Treasurer and Albert Seiboldt as Vice President.

In 1942 after all lots being taken, the cemetery board purchased a 1/2 acre tract of land to the west of cemetery, being 82 ft. deep making 84 'Lots. This was purchased from Albert and Grace Seiboldt. In 1968 the Cemetery Board turned over all funds and equipment to the Copley Twp. Board of Trustees. Up keep of cemetery is now maintained from Copley Twp. tax funds.

The last addition to the cemetery was purchased from Jerry and Inis King the 17th day of December 1985. The 1.25 acres of land were plotted by Ron Zuck into 176 lots with a circle drive. A plot for veteran's burial and flagpole was included. The American Legion Post 726 of Victoria, Ill. erected the flagpole and mortar. Each Memorial Day they hold military services for those veterans buried in Westfall Cemetery.

MAPS OF THE CEMETERY

On the following page is a map of the cemetery. The cemetery is divided into 3 sections. The old section contains 108 Lots and is divided into Sections 1 to 36. Each Lot in the old section contains 8 plots. The position of each individual grave within a lot is shown at the beginning of each entry in the following text by (1), (2) etc... In many cases not all plots are filled. Facing the cemetery, the numbering of the plots starts on the right hand side of each lot.

When the second addition was added they continued with the plot numbers starting with 109 and ending with 192 but they restarted the Section numbers with 1 to 12.

The third addition is largely un-filled and the numbering of the sections and plots was not available. The graves in this area have been noted at the end of this document.

PRIVATE DIRT ROAD

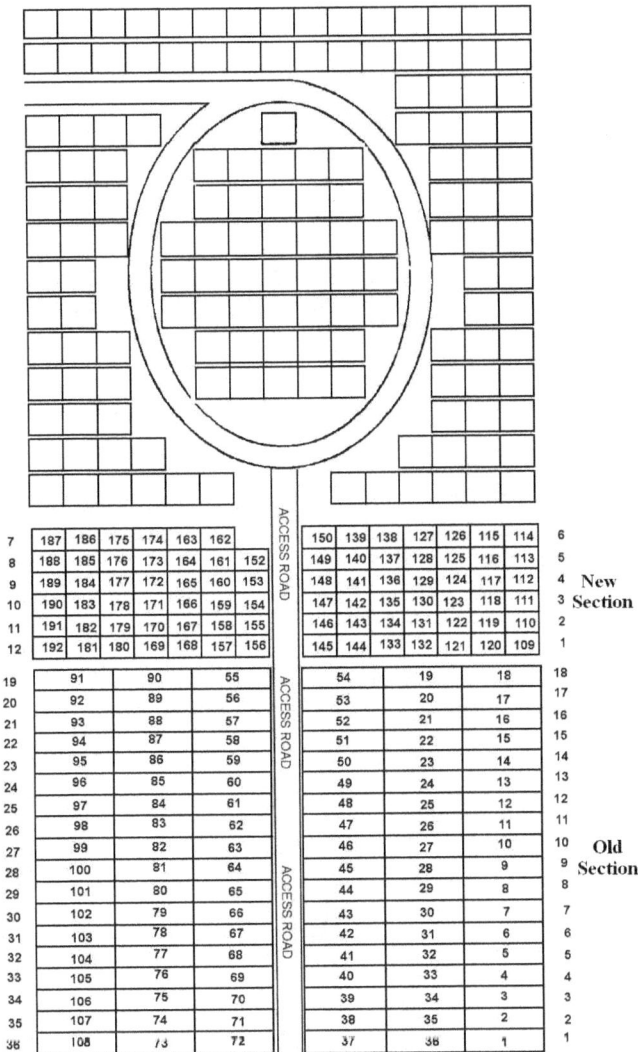

ACCESS ROAD

7	187	186	175	174	163	162		6
8	188	185	176	173	164	161	152	5
9	189	184	177	172	165	160	153	4
10	190	183	178	171	166	159	154	3
11	191	182	179	170	167	158	155	2
12	192	181	180	169	168	157	156	1

New Section

150	139	138	127	126	115	114	6
149	140	137	128	125	116	113	5
148	141	136	129	124	117	112	4
147	142	135	130	123	118	111	3
146	143	134	131	122	119	110	2
145	144	133	132	121	120	109	1

ACCESS ROAD

ACCESS ROAD

19	91	90	55		54	19	18	18
20	92	89	56		53	20	17	17
21	93	88	57		52	21	16	16
22	94	87	58		51	22	15	15
23	95	86	59		50	23	14	14
24	96	85	60		49	24	13	13
25	97	84	61		48	25	12	12
26	98	83	62		47	26	11	11
27	99	82	63		46	27	10	10
28	100	81	64		45	28	9	9
29	101	80	65		44	29	8	8
30	102	79	66		43	30	7	7
31	103	78	67		42	31	6	6
32	104	77	68		41	32	5	5
33	105	76	69		40	33	4	4
34	106	75	70		39	34	3	3
35	107	74	71		38	35	2	2
36	108	73	72		37	36	1	1

Old Section

ACCESS ROAD

FRONT AREA/CEMETERY ENTRANCE

19	91	90	55		54	19	18	18
20	92	89	56		53	20	17	17
21	93	88	57		52	21	16	16
22	94	87	58		51	22	15	15
23	95	86	59		50	23	14	14
24	96	85	60		49	24	13	13
25	97	84	61		48	25	12	12
26	98	83	62		47	26	11	11
27	99	82	63		46	27	10	10
28	100	81	64		45	28	9	9
29	101	80	65		44	29	8	8
30	102	79	66		43	30	7	7
31	103	78	67		42	31	6	6
32	104	77	68		41	32	5	5
33	105	76	69		40	33	4	4
34	106	75	70		39	34	3	3
35	107	74	71		38	35	2	2
36	108	73	72		37	36	1	1

ACCESS ROAD

OLD SECTION - NEAR FRONT OF CEMETERY

CEMETERY ENTRANCE

XII

NEW SECTION - MIDDLE OF CEMETERY

Top Section

Row							
6	114	115	126	127	138	139	150
5	113	116	125	128	137	140	149
4	112	117	124	129	136	141	148
3	111	118	123	130	135	142	147
2	110	119	122	131	134	143	146
1	109	120	121	132	133	144	145

CCESS ROAD

Bottom Section

Row							
7	187	186	175	174	163	162	152
8	188	185	176	173	164	161	153
9	189	184	177	172	165	160	154
10	190	183	178	171	166	159	155
11	191	182	179	170	167	158	156
12	192	181	180	169	168	157	

LAYOUT INFORMATION SOURCES

The source for the layout information for the cemetery is based on the following:

- ➢ Knox County Historical Society's cemetery listing at the Galesburg library.
- ➢ Actual Sexton Plot Layout Records
- ➢ Videos of the headstones taken in 1991 and 2008.
- ➢ Still shots of the headstones taken in 2003.
- ➢ Corrections from obituaries and death certificates.

Although to date, the Knox County cemetery list has been the most valuable resource, it only accounts for the visible stones in the cemetery.

The actual plot layout records show 682 graves that are either filled or designated for specific individuals. In addition, the layout gives 3 place dates in most cases and it also provided some family information. Names are spelled the way they were spelled in the original plot record.

The following pages contain the layout information just as it was in the original layout records along with notes on discrepancies found, conflicting information and various genealogical notes.

In cases where it shows "d.____", the grave is unfilled or the death date was not recorded in the layout records. For graves with no stone it will show (NS). Abbreviations for son of, daughter of, father of, wife of, husband of and mother of are s/o, d/o, f/o, w/o, h/o and m/o respectively. In cases where the plot number is shown as (*), it means a shared plot arrangement.

WESTFALL CEMETERY – OLD SECTION

This is a revised cemetery list based on the Knox County Genealogical Society record dated July 24, 1976 and the Cemetery Sexton records as of April 1997 and observations up to 2008 by Michael T. Osler.

Original Cemetery - 84 Lots

Section 1, Lot 1, Plots 1-8 Lot Owner - John A. Cherrington

(2) **Maxey,** Catherine Dempsey w/o 1. S. A. Webb 2. J. W. Maxey,
      b . 03/17/1807, d. 11/25/1891
(3) **Webb,** Simon A., b. 04/26/1818, d. 08/1/1845
(5) **Pine,** Nellie E. Pine, b. 8/11/1927, d. 8/20/1989, m. 1/6/1947
(6) **Pine,** Raymond M. Pine, b. 6/17/1919, d. 9/1/1995
(7) **Young,** Murel E., b. 9/11/1922, d. 7/28/2003
(8) **Young,** Jesse, b. 5/28/1916, d. 9/24/1990
(8) **Young,** Lyle Allen , b. 1/29/1955, d. 1/29/1955

- Catherine and Simon are on one stone, Nellie and Raymond are on one stone, Murel and Jessie are on one stone.

Section 2, Lot 2, Plots 1-4 Lot Owner - Edward Phillips

(1) **Phillips,** Edward, b. 1845, d. 4/10/1893, Co. E. 83 ILL Rg., Capt.,
(2) **Phllips,** Silence, Phillips, 1847, "?" in plot record (NS)

Section 2, Lot 2, Plots 5-8 Lot Owner - John Rigg

(5) **Smith,** Wilbert Benjamin (Father), b. 3/14/1905, d. 8/22/1954
(6) **Rigg,** Elizabeth Irene Dawson w/o Smith & J.H. Rigg,
      b. 4/27/1884, d. 4/22/1939
(7) **Rigg,** John Henry, b. 4/12/1870, d. 11/29/1931

- Elizabeth and John are on one stone. Plot record shows Elizabeth's birth year as 1884, stone reads 1885.

Section 3, Lot 3, Plots 1-4, Lot Owner - N. C. Eiker

Section 3, Lot 3, Plots 5-8 Lot Owner - Isaac Eiker

(5) **Eiker,** Elizabeth Fields, b. 4/29/1858, d. 12/4/1944

(6) Eiker, Nels C., b. 1/1/1847, d. 1/17/1936
(7) Eiker, Isaac E., b. 2/20/1883, d. 10/27/1909

- Elizabeth and Nels are on one stone. Plot record for Isaac shows d. 10/27/1909, headstone reads 1907. Elizabeth's obit, shows, 4/21, plot record & headstone show 4/29. Her name is Eliza on the stone.

Section 4, Lot 4, Plots 1-4 Lot Owner - Richard V. Wyman

(1) Wyman, Mary Icel Wyman d/o R.V. & A.E., b. 10/11/1883, d. 2/2/1884 (stone unreadable)

Section 4, Lot 4, Plots 5-8 Lot Owner - Charles Dawson

(5) Dawson, Charles William (Father), b. 5/1/1864, d. 12/28/1930
(6) King, Ada (Addie) Agnes Rigg wf of Dawson & King, b. 3/9/1868, d. 9/25/1950
(7) Dawson, Paul Lester, b. 7/1/1887, d. 2/21/1927

Section 5, Lot 5, Plots 1-4 Lot Owner - Benjamin Dawson

(1) Dawson, Benjamin Gerald, b. 4/2/1890, d. 3/23/1964
(2) Dawson, Cecila Amanda Chingren, b. 9/23/1892, d. 1/16/1971
(3) Slutz, Oral, b. 1902, d. 1902 (small stone with Oral on top)
(4) Slutz, Liddie Eva, b. 1908, d. 1908 (stone reads Baby Slutz)

- Benjamin and Cecila are on one stone

Section 5, Lot 5, Plots 5-8 Lot Owner - Clark Slutz

(7) Standiford, Infant, b. 1861, d. 1861 (stone reads Baby)

Section 6, Lot 6, Plots 1-4 Lot Owner - Scott Mundwiler

(2) Mundwiler, Winfield Scott , b. 11/15/1853, d. 11/22/1930
(3) Mundwiler, Fanny Ward w/o W., b. 12/17/1865, d. 9/21/1920
(4) Mundwiler, Le Roy s/o S. & F., b. 1/27/1888, d. 3/26/1888

- Winfield and Fanny are on one stone. LeRoy's stone is broken.

Section 6, Lot 6, Plots 5-8 Lot Owner - E. W. Coleman

(6) Coleman, Twin #1, b. 1/16/1940, d. 1/16/1940 (unmarked stone)

(7) Coleman, Twin #2, b. 1/16/1940, d. 1/16/1940 (unmarked stone)

Section 7, Lot 7, Plots 1-4 Lot Owner - Ernst Steffen

(2) Steffen, Ernst Jacob Steffen, b. 8/23/1859, d. 11/23/1940,
   Born in Bobsdorf Per Prob Stej Holstein, Germany
(4) Steffen, Alice Elizabeth Wyman w/o E.J., b. 3/18/1860,
   d. 9/8/1914, born Persifer Twp., Knox Co., ILL

- Ernst and Alice are on one stone

Section 7, Lot 7, Plots 5-8 Lot Owner - Arthur Wyman

(6) Wyman, Anna Salts w/o A., b. 6/1/1807, d. 1/10/1884
(7) Wyman, Arthur, b. 2/5/1807, d. 5/18/1875

Section 8, Lot 8, Plots 1-8 Lot Owner - Doak Ward

(3) Ward, Isaac, b. 1828, d. 1911
(4) Ward, Mary Wrightman Ward w/o I., b. 7/7/1828, d. 8/15/1887,
   59 yrs, 1 mo, 8 dys
(6) Ward, Miles W. s/o I. & M., b. 3/6/1871, d. 10/23/1873
(7) Ward, Josiah, s/o I. & M., b. 9/6/1868, d. 3/30/1871 (NS)
(8) Ward, Henry, s/o I. & M., b. 10/5/1869, d. 10/7/1869 (NS)

Section 9, Lot 9, Plots 1-8 Lot Owner - A. W. Mitchell

(5) Mitchell, Freddie W., b. 5/30/1877, d. 7/13/1879
(6) Mitchell, Hughie Alexander, b. 12/29/1883, d. 7/8/1888

- The 3 place dates for these two graves came from research done by
   Colleen Adair Taylor. The years are from the headstones.

Section 10, Lot 10, Plots 1-5 Lot Owner - Dave Davis

(1) Davis, David Burton (Father), b. 12/27/1900, d. 7/29/1944
(2) Davis, Linda Hildur Sunberg (Mother), b. 4/29/1891,
   d. 12/10/1970
(3) Davis, Doris Lavon, Twin of David Leo, b. 1/19/1933,
   d. 1/21/1933
(4) Davis, Leslie Earl s/o David & Linda, b. 8/24/1929, d. 8/24/1929

Section 10, Lot 10, Plots 6-9 Lot Owner - Harvey Mitchell

(6) Mitchell, Rufus E. s/o R.H. & A.M., b. 2/20/1877, d. 11/22/1878

Section 11, Lot 11, Plots 1-4 Lot Owner - David Leo Davis

(1) Davis, David Leo, s/o David Burton b. 1/19/1933, d. _____
(2) Davis, Arlean L., b. 9/24/1938, d. 9/4/2005

- David and Arlean are on one big stone with "Parents of David, Vencon, Kathryn", married 11/10/1956. David is the twin brother of Doris.

Section 11, Lot 11, Plots 5-8 Lot Owner - Royal Goff

(6) Goff, Daniel M. s/o R.F. & H.N. or N.N., b. 3/11/1868
       d. 7/11/1868, stone partially buried, age 4 mo

Section 12, Lot 12, Plots 1-8 Lot Owner - James McBeth

(3) McBeth, Gardner, b. 2/8/1870, d. 11/11/1953
(4) McBeth, Hugh b. 8/22/1861, d. 12/20/1940
(7) McBeth, James M., b. 1820, d. 1896
(8) McBeth, Jane w/o J., 54 yrs, 7 mos., b. 11/20/1829, d. 6/20/1884

- Martha and Hugh on one stone; James and Jane on one stone.

Section 13, Lot 13, Plots 1-4 Lot Owner - Fred Clark

(2) Clark, Infant Son (NS), b. 7/18/1921, d. 7/19/1921
(3) Clark, Darlene (NS), b. 9/26/1925, d. 9/27/1925

Section 13, Lot 13, Plots 5-8 Lot Owner - Frank Booth

(7) Booth, Edith d/o F. & A., b. 12/28/1891, d. 4/18/1892

Section 14, Lot 14, Plots 1-8 Lot Owner - S. A. Westfall

(1) Leazenby, Anna Mae Westfall w/o Linzy, b. 5/5/1899,
       d. 1/30/1924
(2) Westfall, Linley Earl, b. 10/16/1895, d. 5/14/1958
                (ILL. PFC Co. K 55 Inf. 7th Div. WW1)
(3) Westfall, George V., b. 4/3/1911, d. 12/3/1974
(4) Westfall, Samuel Ashton (Father), b. 1/7/1865, d. 3/4/1943

(5) Westfall, Ruth Elizabeth Harpman (Mother), b. 12/12/1868, d. 3/25/1934

(6) Westfall, Herbert s/o S. A. & R.E. Westfall, twin of George, b. 4/3/1911, d. 4/3/1911

(7) Sloan, Lullia A. d/o W.H. & M.G. Sloan, b. 7/31/1912, d. 7/31/1912

Section 15, Lot 15, Plots 1-3 Lot Owner - William Charnock

(1) Charnock, Joseph Jr., b. 3/13/1884, d. 9/15/1918
(2) Charnock, Mary Fish, b. 2/3/1843, d. 3/20/1922
(3) Fish, William, b. 2/12/1846, d. 9/2/1927

- Mary's headstone reads 1848, plot record reads 1843. The 1920 census shows her age as 78 which would agree with 1843 as her birth year. Joseph's stone reads b. 1841, plot records shows 1884.

Section 15, Lot 15, Plots 4-8 Lot Owner - Nicholas Blackledge

(4) Blackledge, Mary Jane Charnock , b. 8/16/1885, d. 6/11/1950
(5) Blackledge, Nicholas C., b. 1882, d. 2/5/1959
(6) Blackledge, Infant, b. 2/16/1905, d. 2/16/1905, (NS)

- Mary and Nicholas are on one stone. The infant is buried in the same lot as Mary and Nicholas.

Section 16, Lot 16, Plots 1-4 Lot Owner - Robert B. Morgan

(1) Morgan, Robert Burns, b. 7/22/1883, d. 10/8/1968
(2) Morgan, Clarice Irene Westfall, b. 1/3/1903, d. 8/10/1975
(3) Morgan, Ned H., b. 7/8/1939, d. 2/21/1987, SP4 U.S. Army Vietnam Am. Leg.
(4) Morgan, Robert Burns Jr., b. 10/28/1936, d. 10/28/1936

- Robert Burns birth is 1883 on the plot record but 1888 on the Headstone, Robert and Clarice are on one stone.

Section 16, Lot 16, Plots 5-8 Lot Owner - Ray Spurgon

(7) Spurgon, Infant girl, b. 5/27/1921, d. 5/27/1921 (NS)

Section 17, Lot 17, Plots 1-8 Lot Owner - George Warrensford

5

(1) Swanson, Lois C., b. 8/23/1928, d. 2/8/2006
(1) Swanson, John A. , b. 10/8/1927, d. ____, Vet Korea
(2) Warrensford, Elsie E. Johnson, b. 11/30/1894, d. 4/6/1972
(3) Warrensford, James C., b. 7/5/1900, d. 1/3/1986
(5) Warrensford, Mable P., b. 4/29/1893, d. 4/10/1942
(6) Warrensford, Victoria Taylor w/o G.W., b. 2/17/1870, d.
   7/16/1928
(7) Warrensford, George Washington, b. 12/31/1862, d. 1/29/1937

- Both Swanson's are one stone and it is a new stone. They both
appear to be in plot #1. Actual stone location is estimated. Elsie
and James are on one stone; Victoria and George are on one stone

Section 18, Lot 18, Plots 1-4 Lot Owner - George Horkstrom

(1) Horkstrom, George L., b. 9/1/1884, d. 5/1/1955

- Headstone says Horkstron and it is facing the opposite direction
from the other stones.

Section 18, Lot 18, Plots 5-8 Lot Owner - Charles R. Morgan

(7) Morgan, Charles R., b. 1/20/1906, d. 3/15/1991
(8) Morgan, Annabelle I. Kerns , b. 2/16/1918, d. 2/14/1983

- Both are on one stone.

Section 18, Lot 19, Plots 1-8 Lot Owner - G. Rigg

(1) Lamb, Robert, b. 11/11/1923, d. 7/1/1991
   Stone reads: "The Bird Man, Beloved Husband of Sadie"
(2) Rigg, Garl, b. 9/14/1880, d. 1/13/1975
(3) Rigg, Lucinda Mable Dawson w/o G., b. 1/28/1899 d. 5/2/1954
(5) Rigg, James Arthur s/o G. & L.M., b. 1/6/1924, d. 10/3/1942
(6) Rigg, John E. s/o G. & L.M., b. 1/15/1922, d. 5/10/1940
(7) Rigg, Garl Herbert Jr., b. 1/10/1916, d. 7/27/1983, U.S.
   Army Korea Vietnam
(8) Wall, Nellie M. Rigg (Mom) d/o G. & L.M., b. 1919, d. 1980

- James and John are on one stone. SSN death index shows birth
date for Nellie as 4/15/1919 death date Nov. 1980

Section 17, Lot 20, Plots 1-8 Lot Owner - Charles Johnson

(1) Johnson, Eleanor Mae d/o H.C. & R.A., b. 5/7/1928, d. 5/29/1928
(2) Johnson, Ruth A. Spiegel w/o H.C., b. 8/14/1900, d. 3/6/1975
(3) Johnson, Henry C., b. 11/6/1889, d. 5/15/1964
(5) Johnson, Effie M., b. 7/22/1877, d. 3/15/1878 (NS)
(6) Johnson, Elmer Theodore s/o C.J. & A.C., b. 12/24/1896,
    d. 11/8/1964
(7) Johnson, Charley J. (Father), b. 5/15/1857, d. 11/7/1931
(8) Johnson, Anna Christina Swanson his wife (Mother),
    b. 7/24/1852, d. 6/14/1920

- Ruth and Henry are on one stone, Charley and Anna are on one
stone. Eleanor's headstone reads d. 7/29/1928. Charley's
name on his obituary is Charles G, headstone and plot record
show Charley J.

Section 16, Lot 21, Plots 1-8 Lot Owner - G. S. Westfall

(2) Westfall, Clifford R., b. 12/12/1892, d. 5/31/1971
    ILL. CWT USN WW1
(3) Westfall, Bessie L., b. 9/23/1900, d. 11/23/1974
(4) Westfall, Infant, no stone, most likely Cleo Pearl
(5) Westfall, Mary Eva Dossett w/o George, b. 12/15/1869,
    d. 2/22/1916
(6) Westfall, George Sylvester s/o G. & S., b. 11/28/1858,
    d. 7/12/1938

- Mary and George are on one stone. Infant plot record just says
"No Stone" "Infant Westfall". Per an obituary abstract done by
Ina White Westfall, this is Cleo Pearl, daughter of G.S. and M.
E. d. 1/11/1900, 4 yrs, 11 mos.

Section 15, Lot 22, Plots 1-8 Lot Owner - Art Olson

(4) Olson, Arthur A. s/o M.A. & S.A., b. 12/16/1874, d. 9/18/1948
(5) Olson, Anna S. d/o M.A. & S.A., b. 2/3/1870, d. 9/20/1955
(7) Olson, Sophia Albertina Anderson w/o Matthew, b. 8/24/1839,
    d. 3/21/1917
(8) Olson, Matthew A., born in Sweden, b. 9/8/1837, d. 3/15/1911

- One large stone and 4 small stones, one for each.

Section 14, Lot 23, Plots 1-2 Lot Owner - F. M. Westfall

(1) Westfall, Minnie Sarah England, b. 10/13/1877, d. 12/13/1924
(2) Westfall, Francis (Frank) Marion , b. 6/27/1871, d. 8/27/1948

Section 14, Lot 23, Plots 3-4 Lot Owner - Earl Westfall

(3) Westfall, Odessa Evelyn Needham, b. 3/28/1893, d. 9/27/1980
(4) Westfall, Vera E., b. 5/31/1908, d. 2/1/1955

Section 14, Lot 23, Plots 5-8 Lot Owner - Henry Wyman

(8) Wyman, Oscar s/o H. & S.A., b. 2/2/1892, d. 2/6/1892

Section 13, Lot 24, Plots 1-4 Lot Owner - William Sloan

(1) Sloan, William H., b. 2/4/1894, d. 1/2/1958
(2) Sloan, Myrtle Grace Westfall, b. 3/31/1894, d. 6/22/1982

- Both on one stone.

Section 13, Lot 24, Plots 5-8 Lot Owner - Earl Neff

(5) Frazier, Maurice J. , b. 5/14/1934, d. _____
(6) Frazier, Nancy J. Neff, b. 10/17/1935, d. 3/31/1988
(7) Neff, Jennie Marie Westfall, b. 5/23/1901, d. 4/13/1954
(8) Neff, Earl Allen, b. 8/21/1905, d.12/16/1991

- Maurice and Nancy on one stone, Jennie and Earl on one stone.

Section 12, Lot 25, Plots 1-8 Lot Owner - J. J. Patton

(4) Eldridge, (Infant son) s/o J.E. & M.E., b. 2/15/1893, d. 2/15/1893
(6) Patton, John Delbert s/o J.J. & C.L., b. 11/9/1883, d. 2/20/1951
(7) Patton, Clara L. Taylor (Mother), b. 1/16/1858, d. 9/23/1934
(8) Patton, John J. (Father), b. 10/14/1850, d. 3/23/1920

- One large stone for Patton and 3 small stones as markers.

Section 11, Lot 26, Plots 1-5 Lot Owner - Bane Mitchell

(1) Mitchell, Mary Celica Cherrington, b. 5/30/1863, d. 2/20/1954
(2) Mitchell, Sylvanus (Bane) Enos, b. 3/2/1855, d. 4/9/1917
(3) Mitchell, George Oscar, b. 3/15/1893, d. 10/31/1964

(4) Mitchell, Dellivan G., b. 12/6/1897, d. 7/15/1981

(5) Mitchell, Gladys E., b. 9/14/1890, d. 9/14/1890 (NS)

Section 11, Lot 26, Plots 6-9 Lot Owner - Lewis Mitchell

(7) Mitchell, Elizabeth Reeves Westfall, b. 3/31/1826, d. 11/29/1900

(8) Mitchell, Lewis, b. 12/31/1807, d. 1/9/1888

(9) Mitchell, Fannie C. d/o L. & E.R., b. 4/13/1861, d. 4/3/1862

- Elizabeth's stone and obit. show her birth as 3/19/1826, plot record shows 3/31/1826. Fannie's name is spelled Fanny on her headstone, Fannie on the plot record. All three are on one large stone.

Section 10, Lot 27, Plots 1-3 Lot Owner - John Newberg

(1) Newberg, Augusta Evaline Westfall w/o John, b. 1/7/1868, d. 9/18/1907

(2) Newberg, John M., b. 5/10/1858, d. 3/5/1922

(3) Newberg, Clarence W., b. 5/27/1900, d. 9/28/1975 Pvt. U.S. Army WWII

- Augusta and John are on one stone. Augusta Evaline's death certificate shows she died on 9/22/1907. Plot record shows 9/18/1907 but there is also an arrow pointing to the plot record, with a caption that reads, "Bible Says 2 Sept. 1904"

Section 10, Lot 27, Plots 4-8 Lot Owner - George Westfall

(4) Westfall, Elsie M., b. 1897, d. 1897 and Edgar O., b. 1896, d. 1896. daughter and son of F. & M., on one stone.

(5) Westfall, Susan #2 Bailey, b. 1/29/1825, d. 3/24/1896 "Gone But Not Forgotten", on same stone with George.

(6) Westfall, George, b. 11/17/1811, d. 8/9/1894

(7) Westfall, William Nathan, b. 12/12/1856, d. 10/4/1921

(8) Westfall, Alexander, b. 8/27/1784, d. 12/17/1862, ae 78yr 8m 22d

Section 9, Lot 28, Plots 1-8 Lot Owner - T. M. Patton

(1) Patton, Florence Irene, b. 1887, d. 1887 (NS)

(3) Patton, Sarah Grace d/o H.T. & M.E., b. 8/3/1874, d. 5/9/1876, 1yr., 9m,.6d.

(4) Patton, Mary E. w/o H.T., b. 1/26/1849, d. 4/1/1876, 27yr,2m,5d.

(5) Patton, Carrie b. 2/23/1885, d. 11/4/1886 (NS)
(6) Patton, Thomas M., b. 12/22/1815, d. 1/9/1892, 78yrs. 17d.
(7) Patton, Sally M. w/o T., b. 3/28/1816, d. 5/9/1876,
        60yrs. 1m. 11d.

- Sarah and Mary are on one stone.

Section 8, Lot 29, Plots 1-8 Lot Owner - John Wyman

(6) Wyman, Catherine Mundwiler, b. 7/4/1844, d. 3/18/1912
(7) Wyman, John, b. 7/25/1830, d. 1/3/1904
(8) Wyman, Hannah Taylor 1st w/o John, b. 10/1/1836, d. 4/8/1864

- Catherine, John and Hannah Wyman, are all on the same stone.
  Catherine is John's second wife.

Section 7, Lot 30, Plots 1-8 Lot Owner - Edward J. Wyman

(2) Wyman, William P., b. 8/18/1862, d. 1/11/1918
(3) Wyman, Susan Elizabeth Bradford, w/o Edward, (Mother)
        b. 11/24/1837, d. 9/19/1909
(4) Wyman, Edward J., (Father) h/o Susan, b. 1/10/1833, d. 2/3/1903
(5) Eiker,   Mary Ann Wyman, w/o N. b. 11/25/1858, d. 11/16/1876,
        17yrs., 11m, 21d.
(5) Eiker,   Infant s/o N & M.W. d. 11.16/1876
(6) Wyman, Minerva J., b. 2/26/1870, d. 1/12/1908
(7) Wyman, Oskar S., b. 7/20/1863, d. 4/20/1865,
(8) Wyman, Lincoln H., b. 8/3/1864, d. 10/21/1865, ae 1yr 2m 18d,

- Susan and Edward on one stone. Mary Eiker's infant has the
  same death date as she does and he is in the same plot. Oskar and
  Lincoln's stones are barely readable.

Section 6, Lot 31, Plots 1-8 Lot Owner - Wyman

(6) Wyman, Stephen (Father), b. 6/21/1834, d. 1/18/1914
(7) Wyman, Viola d/o S. & C., b. 10/25/1867, d. 8/3/1868, ae 9m 18d
(8) Wyman, Catherine Minor w/o Stephen (Mother), b. 12/12/1837
        d. 6/5/1868, 30yrs. 7m.

Section 5, Lot 32, Plots 1-9 Lot Owner - Noah Clark Dawson

(*) Dawson, William Clarence, b. 1/24/1903, d. 1/24/1903

(*) Dawson, Ervin Mearl, b. 10/23/1884, d. 10/23/1884
(*) Dawson, Nellie Pearl, b. 9/15/1877, d. 9/15/1877
(*) Dawson, Esta Vearl, b. 1/22/1883, d. 1/22/1883
(4) Dawson, Noah Clark, b. 1/2/1828, d. 6/4/1904
(5) Dawson, Minerva Wyman w/o N.C., b. 9/17/1831, d. 3/13/1907
(6) Dawson, Levi McLellan, b. 10/11/1862, d. 10/7/1886
(7) Dawson, Emma F. Reece w/o L.M., b. 2/13/1871, d. 1/2/1890
(8) Dawson, Edward O., b. 1/17/1851, d. 4/22/1869, ae 18yr 8m 3d

- William, Ervin, Nellie and Esta are sharing plots 1, 2, & 3. Noah and Minerva are on one stone, Levi and Emma are on one stone.

Section 4, Lot 33, Plots 1-4 Lot Owner - William Childress

(2) Childress, William Alinzo, b. 5/5/1868, d. 6/20/1942
(3) Childress, Anna Irene Dawson , b. 10/19/1871, d. 11/23/1942

- Both are on one stone.

Section 4, Lot 33, Plots 5-7 Lot Owner - Zachiras Slutz

(5) Slutz, Eva I., b. 8/23/1873, d. 8/7/1948
(6) Slutz, Zachiras, b. 4/5/1847, d. 12/4/1913
(7) Slutz, Lydia Ladora Dawson w/o Z., b. 3/17/1856, d. 1/31/1917

- Zachiras and Lydia are on one stone.

Section 4, Lot 33, Plot 8 Lot Owner - George Wyman

(8) Wyman, Lewis Clark, b. 11/23/1871, d. 2/16/1873

Section 3, Lot 34, Plot 1 Lot Owner - Joseph Snell

(1) Snell, Infant Snell, b. 1883, d. 1883
(1) Snell, Elijah Claypool, b. 4/18/1814, d. 9/28/1893

- Infant and Elijah are both in Plot 1 with no stones.

Section 3, Lot 34, Plot 2-8 Lot Owner - Ira Dawson

(3) Dawson, Edith Malinda Bothwell, b. 5/29/1864, d. 3/26/1929
(4) Dawson, Henry Aquilla, b. 6/13/1860, d. 10/4/1930
(5) Dawson, Ira Earl, b. 8/31/1888, d. 5/12/1951

(6) Dawson, Cora Lee Burch, b. 10/4/1889, d. 12/14/1970
(7) Dawson, Cora Amanda, b. 6/7/1916, d. 6/7/1916 (NS)
(8) Dawson, William Edward, b. 9/20/1914, d. 9/20/1914 (NS)

- Ira and Cora Lee are on one stone.

Section 2, Lot 35, Plots 1-4 Lot Owner - Ervin Arie

(1) Arie, William George, b. 1882 d. 1882 (NS)
(2) Arie, Henry Ervin, s/o G.E. & R.F., b. 8/2/1914, d. 8/9/1926
(3) Arie, Rachel Florence Mitchell, b. 4/16/1888, d. 12/13/1946
(4) Arie, George Ervin, b. 3/2/1887, d. 4/3/1972

- Rachel and George are on one stone.

Section 2, Lot 35, Plots 5-8 Lot Owner - George Arie

(6) Allen, Mildred Irene, b. 2/28/1931, d. 2/28/1931 (NS)
(7) Arie, William C., b. 12/2/1833, d. 10/27/1905 (NS)
(8) Arie, Valera R. Maxey w/o Wm., b. 4/27/1838, d. 12/15/1876,
born in, Hart Co., KY.

Section 1, Lot 36, Plots 1-8 Lot Owner - Jacob England

(3) England, Ida M. d/o Henry & Orpha, b.12/7/1873,
d. 12/29/1873, ae 22d (small stone)
(4) Thompson, E. P., b. 9/12/1831, d. 2/12/1863 (NS)
(5) England, Samantha J., adopted d/o J. & S., b. 9/5/1860,
d. 11/8/1881
(6) England, Susanah Brown, w/o Jacob, b. 12/29/1830,
d. 6/4/1901
(7) England, Jacob, b. 6/1820, d. 2/15/1905

- Susanah and Jacob are on one stone.
- There is an unknown stone where plots 1 & 2 should be. The plot
record is blank.

Section 1, Lot 37, Plots 1-4 Lot Owner - Henry England

(2) England, Ida M., b.1872, d. 1872
(3) England, Orpha Pratt, b. 6/25/1832, d. 1905
(4) England, Henry, b. 4/30/1830, d. 1905

- All three on one stone.

Section 1, Lot 37, Plots 5-8 Lot Owner - Harvey England

(6) England, Harvey Ephram, b. 11/9/1869, d. 8/6/1936
(7) England, Ida M. Wyman, b. 7/13/1872, d. 2/17/1958

- Both on one stone.

Section 2, Lot 38, Plots 1-6 Lot Owner - Otto Sunberg

(1) Sunberg, Mildred, b. 12/24/1922, d. 3/19/1940
(2) Sunberg, Lucy Webb w/o Otto G., b. 1897, d 1984
(3) Sunberg, Otto Gunhard, b. 2/23/1897, d. 11/5/1963
(4) Sunberg, Otto Ivan, b. 4/11/1866, d. 2/22/1941
(5) Sunberg, Bessie Peterson w/o Otto Ivan, b. 2/21/1866,
    d. 8/28/1937
(6) Sunberg, Carl O., b. 2/2/1893, d. 6/7/1925

- Lucy and Otto G. are on one stone, Otto I. and Bessie are on one
stone.

Section 2, Lot 38, Plots 7-9 Lot Owner - A. W. Anthony

(7) Anthony, Sophia Essex w/o Anthony, d. 7/23/1889   (NS)
(8) Anthony, Mildred H., d. 3/12/1872
(9) Anthony, Alexander,W. Pvt. h/o Sophia, d. 3/9/1889,
    Co. A. 33rd Ill. Inf.

Section 3, Lot 39, Plots 1-8 Lot Owner - Jacob England

(5) England, Daniel H. s/o Jacob & Elizabeth, b. 10/14/1879,
    d. 8/22/1890
(6) Childers, Martha Ann England, b. 12/28/1881, d. 12/11/1913
(7) England, Jacob Jr., b. 11/24/1839, d. 11/6/1886
    Co. D. 101 PA. Inft.
(8) England, Infant, b. 1867, d. 1867, no stone, CA on plot record.

- Daniel and Martha are on one stone.

Section 4, Lot 40, Plots 1-8 Lot Owner - Barney Wagher

(1) Wagher, Mabel M., b. 11/21/1899, d. 8/27/1995

(2) Wagher, Victor Wheeler, b. 3/3/1877, d. 11/7/1962
(3) Wagher, Barrent (Barney) G., b. 12/7/1835, d. 4/24/1902
(4) Wagher, Sarah E. Hedberg w/o Barney, b. 1/29/1842,
      d. 11/14/1910
(*) Wagher, Infant Son of Priscilla, b. 9/8/1862, d. 10/1/1862
      (small marker stone)
(*) Wagher, Mark W., b. 1874, d. 1874, (stone reads Mark W.)
(*) Wagher, Fanny E., b. 7/19/1876, d. 7/30/1876
(*) Wagher, Charles H., b. 9/21/1870, d. 8/2/1871
(*) Wagher, William of B. & S.E. (no dates)
(8) Wagher, Priscilla Crouch w/o Barney, b. 6/17/1837,
      d. 9/19/1862, 25yrs. 3m. 2d

- Priscilla and her Infant Son are on one stone. He died 10/1/1862.
- William is on the same stone with Fanny E. and Charles H. with
  no date. William is not on the plot record.
- Barrent and Sarah are on one stone.
- Plots 5, 6 & 7 are shared by Infant son, M.W., Fanny and Charles.
- William may be the infant son and he is on both headstones.

Section 5, Lot 41, Plots 1-4 Lot Owner - Oliver Crouch

(1) Crouch, George Hobart s/o George & Druzilla, b. 12/12/1896,
      d. 5/15/1923, (NS)
(2) Crouch, Druzilla Viola Westfall, b. 2/6/1865, d. 9/11/1940, (NS)
(3) Crouch, George Oliver, b. 7/22/1854, d. 5/14/1934, (NS)
(4) Crouch, Zelia Irene, b. 10/27/1902, d. 1/8/1968 (NS)

Section 5, Lot 41, Plots 5-8 Lot Owner - Jabe Crouch

(5) Crouch, Rebecca A. Westfall, b. 11/26/1822, d. 4/11/1874
(6) Crouch, James W, b. 10/1/1813, d. 11/17/1873
(7) Crouch, S. Elvine d/o J.W. & R., b. 4/15/1860, d. 5/15/1867

- All on one stone. Rebecca is the wife of James W.

Section 6, Lot 42, Plots 1-8 Lot Owner - Ephraim Burret Pratt

(1) Pratt, Ephraim Burret (Father), b. 12/21/1801, d. 4/10/1863,
(2) Pratt, Electa Lane w/o E.B. (Mother), b. 1/1/1814, d. 6/4/1882
(3) Wagher, Patricia A., b. 1934, d. 10/17/1989
(4) Wagher, Stewart, b. 12/28/1927, d. 12/4/2003

- It says "Our Father and Mother" on the Pratt's stone.

Section 7, Lot 43, Plots 1-9 Lot Owner - Abraham Cherrington

(*) **Cherrington**, Minna Permelia d/o A.B. & N.E., b. 4/29/1861,
      d. 6/4/1864, ae 3 y, 1m, 5d.

(*) **Cherrington**, Rachel Emma d/o A.B. & N.E., b. 3/20/1853,
      d. 4/21/1878, (NS)

(*) **Cherrington**, Abraham Marion, b. 10/6/1855, d. 9/22/1857, (NS)

(*) **Bricker**, Abraham, b. 12/12/1860, d. 9/17/1861

(4) **Cherrington**, Nancy Elizabeth Eldridge w/o A.B., b. 3/10/1830,
      d. 1/6/1879

(5) **Cherrington**, Abraham Bruce, b. 12/25/1826, d. 3/29/1905

(8) **Holm**, Sara Jane Cherrington w/o John, b. 6/26/1850,
      d. 1/16/1880, 29y, 6m, 26d.

- Many of the stones in the group were broken and unreadable.
- Minna, Rachel, Abraham M. and Abraham Bricker are
  sharing plots 1, 2, & 3.
- Nancy and Abraham Cherrington are on one stone.

Section 8, Lot 44, Plots 1-8 Lot Owner - Bruce Cherrington

(2) **Cherrington**, Leven Price s/o A.W. & E.J, b. 5/7/1844,
      d. 12/9/1861

(3) **Cherrington**, Charles s/o A.W. & E.J. b. 7/28/1860, d. 8/30/1860

(4) **Cherrington**, Francis Meryon, b. 2/15/1837, d. 7/26/1873,

(5) **Cherrington**, Rachel Haptonstall, b. 3/9/1807, d. 6/19/1889

(6) **Cherrington**, Bruce, b. 3/15/1801, d. 3/4/1885

(8) **Wagher**, Alfred Vincent, b. 1830, d. 1886, Co. A. 59 Ill.
      Inft., Am. Legion

- Rachel and Bruce are on one stone but barely readable.

Section 9, Lot 45, Plots 1-8 Lot Owner - W. Dawson

(2) **Dawson**, Mandora, d/o J.C. & M.A., b. 8/19/1865, d. 9/14/1866,

(3) **Dawson**, William A., b. 6/24/1838, d. 5/26/1866, ae 27y, 11m, 2d.

(4) **Dawson**, Ada d/o Wm. A., b. 2/27/1866, d. 2/27/1866

(6) **Dawson**, Lovica C. d/o J.C. & M.A., b. 7/28/1850, d. 10/10/1864

(8) **Dawson**, Mary Jane Brown, stone buried, m. 1/27/1841

Section 10, Lot 46, Plots 1-8 Lot Owner - Orlando Lane

(1) Lane, Adaline, d/o O. & A. '?' for dates on plot record
(2) Lane, William, d/o O. & A. '?' for dates on plot record
(3) Lane, Ellen , d/o O. & A.   '?' for dates on plot record
(4) Lane, Orlando h/o Anna, b. 12/20/1819, d. 9/20/1888
(5) Lane, Anna, w/o Orlando (NS)

- Adaline, William, Ellen and Orlando are all on the same stone.
- Plot record shows Orlando was born on 12/19/1819.

Section 11, Lot 47, Plots 1-8 Lot Owner - Enos Mitchell

(4) Mitchell, Enos, b. 3/31/1816, d. 4/22/1859
(5) Mitchell, Harriet N. w/o Enos, b. 6/23/1820, d. 1/1/1865
(7) Burch, Daniel S., b. 10/18/1864, d. 12/3/1941
(8) Burch, Amanda Jane Clayton w/o D., b. 11/27/1862,
        d. 2/9/1919

- Enos and Harriet are on the same stone and an inscription reads
Erected To Their Memory By Their Children 1903"

Section 12, Lot 48, Plots 1-8 Lot Owner - Gardner Eldridge

(1) Eldridge, Augustus F. s/o J. & S., b. 4/27/1867, d. 5/3/1868
(2) Eldridge, Angelina C. d/o J. & S. b. 9/14/1865, d. 5/19/1866
(3) Eldridge, Agnes E., b. 4/3/1859, d. 8/25/1860 (NS)
(6) Chesseman, Elscy A. Eldridge w/o Benjamin E., b. 7/12/1838,
        d. 8/6/1859
(7) Eldridge, Permelia Mecham w/o G., b. 2/17/1800, d. 6/23/1868
(8) Eldridge, Gardner, b. 11/17/1794, d. 1/18/1870

Section 13, Lot 49, Plots 1-8 Lot Owner - Lorenzo Lane

(2) Dawson, Martha d/o S. & M., b. 3/29/1849, d. 10/6/1850
(4) Haptonstall, Charles Inmon s/o W. & C., b. 1/22/1860,
        d. 7/22/1862 ae 2y, 6m
(5) Lane, Amanda Ann d/o L. & J., b. 8/9/1853, d. 9/19/1856
(6) Lane, Euphema d/o L. & J., b. 7/31/1856, d. 9/10/1856

Section 14, Lot 50, Plots 1-8 Lot Owner - M. M. Parkins

(5) Parkins, Eliza d/o M. & M., b. 12/30/1852, d. 2/16/1858

Section 15, Lot 51, Plots 1-8 Lot Owner - Frank Godsil

(3) Godsil, Infant daughter of F. & A., b. 2/13/1918, d. 2/13/1918
(4) Godsil, Francis s/o F. & A.., b. 12/24/1916, d. 2/26/1917
(5) Godsil, Infant daughter of F. &. A., b. 1914, d. 1914
(6) Godsil, Raymond D. Sr. s/o F. & A., b. 1/16/1921, d. 12/20/1981
　　U.S. Navy WWI
(7) Godsil, Esther Mary Siebolt w/o F.P., b. 6/17/1884, d. 6/8/1911
(8) Godsil, Frank P., b. 3/28/1878, d. 10/7/1960

- Frank and Ester are on the same stone.
- Frank's wife Ester died before the children were born.
- The 1930 census shows him married to Anna with some
　of the children..
- Plot record for Esther shows birth in 1885.

Section 16, Lot 52, Plots 1-4   Lot Owner - Samuel Westfall

(3) Westfall, Margarete A. w/o Samuel, b. 10/10/1907, d. 5/21/1994
(4) Westfall, Samuel S., b. 3/11/1906, d. 3/26/1977

- Both are on one stone.

Section 16, Lot 52, Plots 5-8 Lot Owner - Roy Westfall

(5) Sheets, Mildred Eileen Cochran (Mother) wf of Roy
　　Westfall, Blair and Sheets, b. 7/28/1906, d. 9/22/1971
(6) Westfall, Roy A. (Father), b. 5/1/1897, d. 10/3/1951

Section 17, Lot 53, Plots 1-8 Lot Owner - Gus Gilson

(1) Johnson, Margaret G. Gilson d/o Gust & Anna w/o William,
　　b. 10/24/1895, d. 12/22/1969
(2) Johnson, William E. h/o Margaret, b. 4/2/1892, d. 4/1/1962
　　(Am. Leg. Co. B. 7 Eng 5 Dv.)
(3) Mundy, William H., b. 11/13/1918, d. 7/2/1996, Sgt. U.S.
　　Army Air Corps WWII
(3) Mundy, Marian Johnson, b. 5/3/1921, d. _____
(4) Johnson, Bruce H., b. 5/18/1930, d. 12/3/1943
(5) Gilson, Anna Louise Larson w/o Gust, b. 5/23/1867,
　　d. 10/29/1952
(6) Gilson, Gust Adolph h/o Anna, b. 6/27/1871, d. 1/19/1950
(7) Gilson, Harold Leroy, b. 3/15/1903, d. 2/10/1920

(8) Gilson, Helen Alvira, b. 8/11/1900, d. 2/11/1920
(9) Gilson, Alfred Rudolph, b. 9/13/1897, d. 2/11/1920

- The Mundy plots are not on this version of the plot record.
  It appears that they are both in Plot 3, since it is the only
  open plot between William and Bruce Johnson.
- William H. and Marian have one stone.
- Plot record shows Helen Alvira, but headstone reads Helen E.
- Alfred Rudolph's headstone reads Rudolph A.

Section 18, Lot 54, Plots 1-4 Lot Owner - Gus Johnson

(1) Johnson, Marie Estelle, b. 3/4/1904, d. 11/14/1982
(2) Johnson, Lottie M. Montgomery, b. 8/9/1883, d. 1/3/1956
(3) Johnson, Gust A., b. 6/5/1883, d. 5/10/1962

- Lottie and Gust are on one stone. The name is spelled Gust on
  the plot record and headstone, but Guss in the obituary.

Section 18, Lot 54, Plots 5-8 Lot Owner - Andrew Nelson Jr.

(5) Nelson, Andrew Jr. b. 1855 d. 1874 (small stone)

Section 19, Lot 55, Plots 1-4 Lot Owner - Otto Horkstrom

(1) Horkstrom, Otto, b. 3/27/1881, d. 3/1/1959
(2) Horkstrom, Selma Othelio Moberg, b. 2/27/1874, d. 8/5/1956
(3) Rundle, Evelyn A. Horkstrom, b. 2/12/1907, d. 9/29/1983
(4) Rundle, Raymond O., b. 10/21/1903, d. 11/2/1966

- Otto and Selma are on one stone, Evelyn and Raymond are on
  one stone.

Section 19, Lot 55, Plots 5-8 Lot Owner - Mrs. John Little

(7) Little, Millie E. Colwell (Mother), b. 10/29/1890, d. 4/13/1968
(8) Little, John Monroe (Father), b. 3/28/1883, d. 1/6/1945

- One new stone for both

Section 20, Lot 56, Plots 1-8 Lot Owner - Swan Peter Ecklund

(2) Ecklund, Ellen J. Johnson w/o S. P., b. 12/4/1846, d. 11/27/1907

(3) Ecklund, Swan Peter Ecklund, b. 7/8/1854, d. 8/18/1932
(4) Ecklund, William E., b. 11/28/1884, d. 4/2/1942 (NS)

- Ellen and Swan are on one stone.

Section 21, Lot 57, Plots 1-4, Lot Owner - Eric Newberg

(1) Newberg, Eric J., b. 12/24/1814, d. 7/5/1899, ae 84yr 6m 11d
(2) Newberg, Martha Larson w/o E. J., b. 2/22/1831, d. 1/23/1875
(3) Newberg, Frank, b. 7/22/1866, d. 11/17/1882, ae 16yr 3m 25d

- All three on one stone. Plot records shows Newburg but headstone reads Newberg.

Section 21, Lot 57, Plots 5-8 Lot Owner - George Newberg

(6) Brown, Robert C., b. 9/24/1931, d. 6/27/2005
(7) Brown, Darlos Y. w/o Robert, b. 11/13/1935, d. 10/30/1988,
    m. 8/13/1969
(8) Newberg, George L., b 1/7/1861, d. 4/2/1935 (NS)

- Robert and Darlos are on one stone. At base of stone under Robert C. it says "Buried in Oneida Cemetery".

Section 22, Lot 58, Plots 1-2 Lot Owner - Olof Moberg

(1) Moberg, Betsey w/o Olof, b. 1/12/1812, d. 8/5/1899
(2) Moberg, Olof, b. 12/10/1809, d. 4/2/1871, ae 62yr 3m 22d, (NS)

Section 22, Lot 58, Plots 3-8 Lot Owner - Nellie Westergreen

(3) Westergreen, Betsey O. Moberg, b. 7/7/1842, d. 11/18/1916
(4) Westergreen, Swan O., b. 3/19/1839, d. 1/7/1910
(5) Westergreen, Nellie Christine, d/o Thomas, b. 2/25/1867,
    d. 5/18/1951,
(7) Pratt, Gustaf Jr., d. 2/8/1876

- The original plot record for plot 7, reads Gustaf Brott Jr. The library list showed it as Pratt born in Sweden and on the headstone it looked like Augusta Pratt, but it was hard to read.

Section 23, Lot 59, Plot 1 Lot Owner - Gardner A. Cherrington

(1) Cherrington, Gardner Allen s/o S. & S.S., b. 10/3/1855,
d. 3/17/1871

Section 23, Lot 59, Plots 2-5 Lot Owner - Alfred Stevens

(2) Stevens, Alfred Clyde (Father), b. 11/11/1887, d. 10/2/1949
(3) Stevens, Eva Elizabeth Cherrington w/o Alfred (Mother),
b. 8/26/1886, d. 8/26/1966
(4) Stevens, Donald Loren s/o A.C. & E.E , b. 10/30/1920,
d. 9/18/1927
(5) Stevens, Geneva Pearl d/o A.C. & E.E., b. 5/18/1908,
d. 11/18/1919

- Alfred and Eva are on one stone.
- Donald's Obit. says his middle name is Warren, the
headstone and plot record read Loren.

Section 23, Lot 59, Plots 6-8 Lot Owner - Austin King

(6) King, Wesley Gardner s/o C. & P., b. 4/15/1920, d. 11/24/1921
(7) King, Leslie Delbert , b. 3/28/1916, d. 11/13/1971
(8) King, Ethel Laver King, b. 3/5/1917, d. 6/25/1987
(*) King, Baby, d. 10/18/1936

- Baby King is buried b/t Wesley and Leslie
- Leslie and Ethel are on one stone.

Section 24, Lot 60, Plots 1-8 Lot Owner - Lewis Peterson

(1) Stinson, James E. s/o A. & S., b. 2/2/1859, d. 2/2/1859
(2) King, Charles C. h/o Clara, b. 7/9/1909, d. 8/23/1997
m. 10/15/1929
(3) King, Clara I. (Wagher) w/o Charles C., b. 2/18/1906,
d. 8/16/1999, m. 10/15/1929
(6) Peterson, Lewis (Lars), b. 4/29/1816, d. 1/28/1909
(7) Peterson, Anna w/o L., b. 12/18/1808, d. 12/6/1886

- Charles and Clara are on one stone, Lewis and Anna are on
one stone.

Section 25, Lot 61, Plots 1-8 Lot Owner - England

(4) Ponder, Martin, b. 8/7/1909, d. 9/5/1993
(5) Ponder, Glyda M. w/o Martin, b. 7/24/1915, d. 3/25/1994
(6) England, John Dempsey, b. 6/2/1874, d. 11/9/1961
(7) England, Mary Ann Eiker w/o J. D., b. 11/10/1880, d. 10/22/1975
(8) England, Lyda d/o J. D. & M., b. 7/24/1915, d. 7/26/1915

- Martin and Glyda are on one stone, John and Mary are on one stone.
- Lyda's name is spelled Lydia on the plot record and Lyda on the
headstone. The library listing and the plot record show her
b. 7/29/1916 d. 8/2/1916. Her headstone reads b. July 24,
1915 d. July 26, 1915. Her headstone also says twin sister to
Glyda, who was born on July 24, 1915.

Section 26, Lot 62, Plots 1-3 Lot Owner - Floyd Wagher

(1) Wagher, Rosemary w/o Floyd, b. 3/18/1924, d. 6/23/1987
(2) Wagher, Floyd, b. 12/7/1904, d. 12/3/1990

Section 26, Lot 62, Plots 4-8 Lot Owner - Glenn England

(5) England, G. Glen, b. 3/1/1908, d. 12/1/1997
(6) England, Ruth S., b. 9/29/1911, d. 6/14/1994
(7) England, Harold E., b. 8/22/1941, d. 8/22/1941 (Infant)

- All three England's above are on the same stone.

Section 27, Lot 63, Plots 1-8 Lot Owner - Bert Wagher

(1) Wagher, Infant Son s/o B.G. & H.C., b. 3/4/1912, d. 3/4/1912
(2) Wagher, Everet Vernon s/o B.G. & H.C., b. 11/28/1918,
    d. 12/31/1919
(3) Wagher, Harold L. s/o B.G. & H.C., b. 3/24/1907, d. 12/7/1931
(4) Wagher, Constance Rosine w/o Bertis, b. 10/8/1878, d. 8/24/1967
(5) Wagher, Bertis (Bert) Garrett, b. 7/3/1872, d. 11/9/1958
(*) Wagher, Ray R., b. 2/7/1910, d. 11/25/1986, Tec. U.S. Army
    WWII
(6) Wagher, Earl H. (Father), b. 10/27/1908, d. 6/4/1981, Am. Legion
(7) Wagher, Lucille E. Morris (Mother), b. 2/17/1918, d. 11/18/1994
(8) Wagher, Sally Rosine d/o E. H. & L. E., b. 9/7/1941, d. 9/7/1941
(8) Wagher, Judith A. d/o E. H. & L. E., b. 8/3/1940, d. 8/4/1940

- Constance Rosine is also H. C. and on the same stone with
Bertis. The 1910 Census shows Berti and Rosine with Harold

21

L. age 3 and Earl 1, along with the rest of the family.
Children's headstones show son of B.G. and H.C.
- Earl, Lucille, Sally and Judith are all on the same stone. Sally
  and Judith have Dau. above their names on the headstone.
  Sally and Judith are both in Plot # 8.
- Everet's headstone reads d. 1919 the plot record shows d. 1918.
- Ray R. is a new stone in between Bert and Earl. Plot record
  shows no gaps between Bert and Earl.

Section 28, Lot 64, Plot 1 Lot Owner - Swank

(1) **Swank**, Elenor w/o G.W., b. 1/30/1834, d. 1/30/1864, aged 30 yrs.

Section 28, Lot 64, Plots 2-8 Lot Owner - Thomas Westergreen

(2) **Westergreen**, Mable Charlotte Ecklund, b. 7/6/1887,
    d. 11/8/1960 w/o Thomas
(3) **Westergreen**, Thomas Vincent, b. 2/10/1885, d. 12/11/1929
(8) **Westergreen**, Infant, b. 8/17/1916, d. 8/17/1916, (NS)

Section 29, Lot 65, Plots 1-4 Lot Owner - George Wagher

(1) **Wagher**, Ira s/o G.W. & L.E., b. 8/18/1861, d. 9/11/1861, ae 24d

Section 29, Lot 65, Plots 5-9 Lot Owner - Gardner B. Cherrington

(6) **Cherrington**, Infant Girl, b. 8/1/1914, d. 8/1/1914, (NS)
(7) **Cherrington**, Mary Jane Milroy w/o G. B., b. 2/14/1864,
    d. 8/31/1954
(8) **Cherrington**, Gardner Bruce, b. 4/29/1858, d. 5/18/1934
(9) **King**, Pearl J. d/o G. B. & M. J., b. 1/29/1890, d. 2/3/1988

- Mary and Gardner are on the same stone.

Section 30, Lot 66, Plots 1-8 Lot Owner - Charles W. Hapstonstall

(1) **Haptonstall**, C. W., b. 5/15/1801, d. 12/26/1864, (GAR),
    Co. G. 36 ILL. Inft.
(2) **Haptonstall**, Mary A. w/o Jordan, b. 5/22/1825, d. 6/12/1897
(3) **Haptonstall**, Sophrona A. d/o of J. & M. A., b. 8/25/1875,
    d. 9/22/1875, ae 28d

(4) Haptonstall, Tryphena, b. 1868, d. 1868, ae 16d
(5) Haptonstall, J. H. Co. A 58 Rg. ILL. Inft, (no dates)
(6) Haptonstall, William E., b. 1/7/1855, d. 10/30/1897

Section 31, Lot 67, Plots 1-4, Lot Owner - George Flynn

(2) Flynn, George, b. 5/4/1860, d. 3/15/1904, Gone but not forgotten
(3) Flynn, Melvina d/o John, b. 2/27/1862, d. 2/27/1862
(4) Flynn, John Flynn, b. 11/7/1816, d. 11/19/1880, ae 64yr 12d.

- At the base of John's stone it says Baby.

Section 31, Lot 67, Plots 5-8 Lot Owner - John Flynn

(6) Flynn, William S. (Willie) s/o Wm. & M. E., b. 10/28/1866,
    d. 5/5/1882, ae 15 yr. 6m. 7d.
(7) Flynn, John C. s/o Wm. & M., b. 4/9/1869, d. 1/26/1873
(8) Flynn, Infant s/o W. & M., b. 1/31/1868, d. 1/31/1868 (NS)

- All three children and their mother are listed on a large metal
  headstone. The headstone and Mary are in Section 33, Lot 76.
  Mary is listed as Pvt. (Nurse) Mary E. Russell Flynn, on the plot
  record and as Mary E. Flynn, on the headstone. The children are
  actually buried here according to the plot records.
- Inscription on metal stone reads, Gone from Our Home, But
  Not From Our Hearts.

Section 32, Lot 68, Plots 1-4 Lot Owner - Parkins

(1) Parkins, Andrew s/o A. & M., b. 5/2/1865, d. 5/2/1865 (NS)
(2) Parkins, Infant, (unmarked stone)

Section 32, Lot 68, Plots 5-8 Lot Owner - Harvey Rice

(6) Rice, Harvey M., b. 6/22/1865, d. 1/9/1937, (NS)

Section 33, Lot 69, Plots 1-4 Lot Owner - Edward Rice

(1) Rice, Frank D. s/o E. W. & E., b. 4/9/1868, d. 11/30/1868
(2) Rice, Edward W., b. 1/6/1818, d. 7/7/1880
(3) Rice, Elizabeth Westfall w/o E. W., b. 12/14/1841, d. 12/15/1915

- All three on one stone.

- Death Certificate for Elizabeth says she died in 1914.

Section 33, Lot 69, Plots 5-6 Lot Owner - George Rice

(5) Rice, George W., b. 11/9/1875, d. 9/17/1937
(6) Rice, Gertrude Fields w/o George W., b. 4/10/1883, d. 2/27/1981

- Both on one stone.
- Plot record and headstone both show Gertrude's birth as
  1886, Obit shows 1883.

Section 33, Lot 69, Plots 7-8 Lot Owner - James Fields

(7) Fields, James, b. 3/20/1855, d. 1/22/1934
(8) Fields, Hannah Elizabeth Warrensford, b. 11/27/1856,
     d. 9/7/1932

- Plot record for James shows birth 3/20/1855, headstone reads
  1857. Both are on one stone.

Section 34, Lot 70, Plot 1 Lot Owner - Edward Myrick

(1) Myrick, Edward F., b. 6/29/1853, d. 5/30/1860

Section 34, Lot 70, Plots 2-3 Lot Owner - William Fields

(2) Fields, William H., b. 5/23/1846, d. 7/15/1914
(3) Fields, Hannah J. Rigg w/o Wm. H., b. 4/10/1846, d. 12/12/1926

- Both on same stone.

Section 34, Lot 70, Plots 4-8 Lot Owner - John Fields

(4) Fields, John Marshall Sr., b. 10/27/1878, d. 1/6/1937
(5) Fields, Gertrude Jean Davies w/o John, b. 6/27/1891, d. 6/18/1954
(6) Fields, John Marshall Jr. s/o J. & G., b. 3/16/1918, d._____
(7) Fields, Helen Louise Hanson w/o John Jr., b. 9/29/1919, d. ____
(8) Fields, David Lee s/o John & Helen, b. 1/28/1945, d. 1/28/1945

- In the Cemetery layout, John Jr. and Helen are shown in Section 34,
  Lot 70, however they have a stone in the new section of the
  Cemetery, Sec 9 Lot 153 that has their names the inscription "Our
  Children Mary Ann, John, Marsha, Robert", m. 10/25/1942.

Section 35, Lot 71, Plots 1-2 Lot Owner - Charles Byers

(1) Byers, Question Marks for first name and date.
(2) Beyer, Lidora Bell d/o. C. A. & H., b. 8/21/1866, d. 6/6/1875
(small stone)

- The Plot record shows plot 1 with a question mark for the first
name, then Byers and then a question mark for the dates. Plot 2
shows Lidora Beyer with dates.

Section 35, Lot 71, Plots 3-8 Lot Owner - Beverly and/or Stamper Cochran

(3) Cochran, Hedvig Marie Elizabeth Rosine, b. 3/29/1874,
d. 7/24/1945
(4) Cochran, Robert Otis, b. 11/23/1871, d. 11/16/1933
(5) Cochran, Bernetta L., b. 1905, d. 7/3/1932

- Hedvig and Robert are on the same stone.
- Robert's headstone reads b. 1877, the Obit. has 12/23/1876
and the plot record reads 11/23/1871. As of 2008, there is a new
stone that reads 1874.

Section 36, Lot 72, Plots 1-8 Lot Owner - George England Sr.

(1) England, Susannah Webb w/o George (Mother), b. 5/17/1840,
d. 1914
(2) England, George, b. 5/4/1825, d. 1911 (Father)
(3) Newberg, Anna E. England, b. 5/1/1864, d. 12/13/1941
(4) England, Jacob Henry, b. 3/16/1876, d. 12/4/1951
(5) England, Emma Olive Westergreen, b. 1/25/1874, d. 1/12/1974
(8) England, Madison Webb s/o George and Susan Webb,
b. 9/23/1872, d. 2/28/1873

- Susannah and George on one stone, Jacob and Emma on one stone.
- Plot record for Lot 3 reads Anna E.., the Headstone reads
Annie E. and obit. has Anna C.

Section 36, Lot 73, Plots 1-8 Lot Owner - Samuel F. Patton

(1) Patton, Samuel F. b. 3/13/1839, d. 2/18/1893
1st Lt. Co. A. 59 IL. Rg. d., ae 53yr, 11m, 5d.

(2) Patton, Hugh Recruit James , b. 11/22/1842, d. 1/16/1864
  Co. A. 59 Rg. ILL Vol. d., died in Hospital at Louisville,
  Ky., ae 21yr 11m 24d
(3) Patton, William N., b. 1/29/1838, d. 4/9/1921
(5) Patton, Susie May, b. 3/25/1888, d. 7/27/1971, (NS)
(6) Patton, Catherine J. Johnson, b. 5/,5/1853, d. 2/9/1945
(7) Patton, Hugh Thomas, b. 7/7/1848, d. 2/7/1913
(8) Patton, Hugh, b. 6/2/1818, d. 1/9/1893 Co. K, 4 Rg. ILL. Inft.
  Mex. War

- Lt. Samuel and Recruit James are on the same stone.
- William's death date is shown as 4/8 on the library list and
  the headstone. It is shown as 4/9 on the plot record and obituary.

Section 35, Lot 74, Plots 1-8 Lot Owner - William Johnson

(2) Johnson, Elsy w/o B., b. 2/24/1836, d. 6/9/1890
(3) Johnson, Benjamin, b. 9/24/1829, d. no date on stone or plot
(4) Johnson, Juanita (June) Gibbs (Mother), b. 10/16/1872,
  d. 5/26/1933
(5) Johnson, William Henry (Father), b. 4/13/1865, d. 4/18/1934
(6) Johnson, Oscar F., b. 1/10/1894, d. 5/13/1970 Iowa Pvt.
  USA WW1

- Juanita and William are on one stone.
- Elsy and Benjamin on one stone.
- 1880 census shows Benjamin 50, Elsie 44 with children, Willie,
  Chas, Anna, Tilda and Amy.

Section 34, Lot 75, Plots 1-4 Lot Owner - William W. England

(1) England, Lorena M. Taylor, 1st wf of W. W., b. 1/5/1869,
  d. 10/23/1893, ae 24yr. 9m. 18d.
(2) England, William Watson, b. 8/7/1862, d. 5/18/1907
(4) England, Infant Girl, b. 8/26/1923, d. 8/26/1923, (NS)

- Lorena and William are on one stone.

Section 34, Lot 75, Plots 5-8 Lot Owner - David Taylor

(8) Taylor, David, b. 1/12/1828, d. 10/5/1900, ae 72yr. 8m. 23d.

Section 33, Lot 76, Plots 1-5 Lot Owner - C. N. Russell

(1) Russell, Lutecia Cherrington w/o C. N., b. 1/14/1825,
    d. 3/14/1881
(4) Flynn, Mary E. Russell Pvt. Nurse l, b. 7/22/1849, d. 2/22/1888,
    (GAR)

- Mary, Infant, John C. and Willie S. are all listed on this stone
but the children are buried in Section 31, Lot 67.

Section 33, Lot 76, Plots 6-9 Lot Owner - Sanford Wyman

(6) Russell, Charles Neptune, b. 7/2/1820, d. 9/20/1901
(7) Wyman, Sanford, b. 6/7/1866, d. 7/25/1905
(8) Wyman, Fanny Clarine Flynn, b. 1872, d. 1900
(9) Wyman, V., Only question marks for dates on plot record

Section 32, Lot 77, Plots 1-2 Lot Owner - J. Flynn

(1) Flynn, Mary dau. of J. & M., b. 11/30/1847, d. 1/30/1879
(2) Flynn, Benjamin son of J. & M., b. 2/13/1845, d. 3/31/1865,
    died at White Oak, Tenn., Pvt. 83 Rg. .ILL. Vol.

Section 32, Lot 77, Plots 3-8 have no owner

Section 31, Lot 78, Plots 1-8 Lot Owner - Johnson

(3) Johnson, Mary d/o R. & E. P., b. 11/12/1870, d. 10/12/1871
(4) Johnson, Mary, b. 12/2/1869, d. 11/23/1870
(5) Johnson, Emma d/o R. & E.P., b. 9/6/1875, d. 7/23/1878
(6) Johnson, William s/o R. & E.P., b. 11/8/1874, d. 5/23/1879
(7) Flynn,   Joseph (Joe), b. 3/4/1862, d. 8/24/1949
(8) Flynn,   Kate (Katie) Alice Denny, b. 3/28/1871, d. 2/1/1966

- Joseph and Kate Flynn are on one stone.
- Mary d/o R. & E.P. has her own stone.
- Emma and one other child are on the same stone, unreadable.

Section 30, Lot 79, Plots 1-8 Lot Owner - Unknown

(4) Minor, Ada, b. 3/21/1876, d. 4/11/1876
(5) Flynn, Infant, No dates, no stone, buried next to James and Nora.
(6) Flynn, James D. Edwin, b. 8/23/1886, d. 8/6/1951
(7) Flynn, Nora Welling Benedist, b. 8/16/1890, d. 10/19/1975

(8) Flynn, Infant, No dates, no stone, buried next to James and Nora.

- James and Nora are on one stone.
- The plot records for the infants, just say "BABY" with no dates.
- Plot record shows James D. as James Edwin.
- Nora's name of Benedist comes from the plot record.
- Ada Minor may be the same as the Ada Monroe in the Knox Co. Cemetery list.

Section 29, Lot 80, Plots 1-2 Lot Owner - John Peak

(1) Peak, John, d. 6/8/1959 (NS)
(2) Peak, Mable P. Sleutz d/o Charity Jacobs, b. 1884 (NS)

- John has question marks for his birth date in the plot record.
- Mable has question marks for her death date in the plot record.

Section 29, Lot 80, Plots 3-8, Lot Owner - Julius Sleutz

(3) Baughman, Daisy Bell Sleutz w/o De Brian and Baughman, b. 4/28/1895, d. 10/18/1958 (Mother)
(4) Sleutz, Ida, question marks for dates on plot record, (NS)
(5) Sleutz, James Wesley, b. 8/29/1886, d. 1/8/1954, (NS)
(6) Jacobs, b. 7/17/1861, d. 10/4/1903, (NS)
(7) Sleutz, Julius E., b. 1/4/1851, d. 8/9/1916, (NS)
(8) Sleutz, William Harry, b. 1889, d. 6/8/1959 (NS)

Section 28, Lot 81, Plots 1-8 Lot Owner - William J. Oliver

(6) Oliver, Jennie Wagher w/o Wm. J., b. 2/14/1866, d. 2/1/1903, died at Laugley, South Carolina
(8) Wagher, Phillip, b. 11/2/1792, d. 3/21/1883

- Phillip is on the same stone with Johnnie Wagher in Lot 100 but according to the plot record, he is buried here.

Section 27, Lot 82, Plots 1-4 Lot Owner - Eric Horkstrom

(1) Horkstrom, Louisa, b. 10/6/1810, d. 8/4/1886
(2) Horkstrom, Eric, b. 1841, d. 1913
(3) Horkstrom, Carolina Frans, d. 1933, (NS)
(4) Horkstrom, Charles Eric, b. 9/26/1866, d. 3/31/1937, (NS)

Section 27, Lot 82, Plots 5-8 Lot Owner - Otto Horkstrom

(5) Smith, Ellen Frans Horkstrom w/o Flynn 1st, b. 1/6/1872, d. 4/21/1950

(6) Horkstrom, Infant s/o Otto & Selma, b. 1913, d. 1913, (NS)

(7) Horkstrom, Twin to Geo. W., b. 10/4/1905, d. 10/4/1905, (NS)

- The information about the two infants came from the plot record.

Section 26, Lot 83, Plots 1-8 Lot Owner - George Arie

(1) Arie, Effie F. d/o G. & I.B., b. 1/30/1900, d. 1/17/1901

(2) Arie, Ethel J. d/o G.W. & I.B., b. 7/27/1884, d. 2/24/1923

(3) Arie, Ida Bell Myrick w/o George, b. 8/4/1864, d. 5/11/1925

(4) Arie, George W., b. 12/25/1858, d. 8/24/1942

Section 25, Lot 84, Plots 1-4 Lot Owner - Thomas King

(1) Parkins, Baby of H.F. & I.J. Parkins (small stone)

(4) King, Jerol Thomas, b. 9/28/1939, d. 10/3/1939
(Moved to Tulon Cemetery on 5/22/1976)

Section 25, Lot 84, Plots 5-8 Lot Owner - Charles Wagher

(7) Wagher, Agnes L. Luxmore (Mother), b. 5/23/1872, d.11/22/1950

(8) Wagher, Charles (Father), b. 4/4/1861, d. 2/27/1938

Section 24, Lot 85, Plots 1-4 Lot Owner - Nels Norburg

(1) Norburg, Infant Son, b. 4/28/1920, d. 4/28/1920, (NS)

- The plot record just says infant son. It is an assumption that the last name is Norburg because of the name of the lot owner.

Section 24, Lot 85, Plots 5-8 Lot Owner - N. Cochran

(8) Cochran, Victor N., b. 2/8/1879, d. 8/4/1954, (Flag, Am Leg.)

Section 23, Lot 86, Plots 1-8 Lot Owner - Catherine A. Larson

(1) Larson, Albert, b. 4/12/1860, d. 3/8/1880

(2) Larson, John E., b. 11/7/1862, d. 2/29/1884

(3) Larson, William L., b. 1831, d. 1864 (Flag)

(4) Larson, Catherine Ann w/o Wm,.b.1829, d. 1894
(5) Larson, Anna , b. 2/4/1856, d. 3/29/1937, (NS)
(6) Larson, Lewis W., b. 10/19/1858, d. 3/21/1934, (NS)
(8) Larson, George, b. 4/27/1849, d. 2/13/1909

- Albert and John are on one stone, William and Catherine are on one stone.

Section 22, Lot 87, Plots 1-4 Lot Owner - Peter Frans

(1) Frans, Marie P. w/o P., b. 12/16/1802, d. 6/30/1904
(2) Frans, Peter, b. 4/13/1823, d. 4/16/1902
(3) Frans, Mary Weedman, b. 1843, d. 1918

- Marie and Peter are on one stone.

Section 22, Lot 87, Plots 5-8 Lot Owner - Robert E. Cochran

(7) Cochran, Robert E. (Grandpa), b. 1/7/1845, d. 12/13/1931
(8) Cochran, Sophia Frans (Grandma), b. 1/4/1850, d. 4/3/1928

- Robert and Sophia are both on one stone.

Section 21, Lot 88, Plots 1-8 Lot Owner - Charles Trotter

(7) Trotter, Cecil Richard (Husband), b. 1908, d. 1/6/1954
(8) Trotter, Lettie Phoebe Richards w/o Charles, b. 1872, d. 1910
(9) Trotter, Charles, b. 4/27/1865, d. 2/8/1935

- Lettie and Charles are on one stone.

Section 20, Lot 89, Plots 1-8 Lot Owner - Olof Swanson

(4) Swanson, George W., b. 2/26/1899, d. 7/4/1982
(6) Swanson, Edwin Olof, b. 11/17/1900, d. 7/27/1920
(7) Swanson, Emma Burg w/o O. R. , b. 10/24/1872, d. 8/9/1939
(8) Swanson, Olof R., b. 10/30/1873, d. 3/26/1958

- Emma and Olof are on one stone.

Section 19, Lot 90, Plots 1-4 Lot Owner - Merle Wyman

(1) Wyman, Harriett Jane Webb, b. 1/21/1901, d. 2/26/1960

(2) Wyman, Merle Stephen, b. 9/30/1894, d. 2/11/1956
(3) Wyman, Saundra L., b. 6/23/1937, d. _____
(4) Wyman, William J., b. 3/15/1934, d. _____

- Saundra and William were married 12/2/1955 and the stone reads
Our Daughters Billie and Brenda.
- Harriett and Merle are on one stone.

Section 19, Lot 90, Plots 5-8 Lot Owner - Vincil Stevens

(6) Stevens, Vencel, b. 4/8/1911, d. _____
(7) Stevens, Thelma G., b. 8/15/1915, d. 1/22/1999
(8) Stevens, Infant Son, b. 8/4/1944, d. 8/4/1944 (NS)

- All three are on one stone. Plot locations are estimated.

Section 19, Lot 91, Plots 1-4 Lot Owner - Transient

(2) Saline, John, b. 8/10/1868, d. 8/2/1908

Section 19, Lot 91, Plots 5-8 Lot Owner - Gardie Cherrington

(6) Winchel, Madge G. Cherrington w/o Ervin, b. 1944, d._____
(7) Winchel, Ervin L. Sr., b. 9/9/1920, d. 12/21/1981
(8) Phillips, Infant Girl, b. 3/5/1973, d. 3/5/1973, (Martin Fun Mk)
(9) Smith, Vada Mary b. 9/6/1937 d. 6/24/1990

- Madge and Ervin are on one stone.

Section 20, Lot 92, Plots 1-4 Lot Owner - Patrick Cherrington

(1) Cherrington, Viola Pearl Little, b. 7/6/1913, d. 1/24/1940
(2) Cherrington, Patrick Edwin, b. 4/28/1897, d. 11/21/1996
(3) Cherrington, Mary Catherine, b. 3/2/1930, d. 10/28/1949

- Patrick and Viola are on one stone.

Section 20, Lot 92, Plots 5-8 Lot Owner - Gardie Cherrington

(4) Cherrington, Vada Gertrude w/o G. I., b. 1/12/1910, d. 7/2/1988
(5) Cherrington, Gardner Ira, b. 11/29/1893, d. 2/10/1971, (PFC. 11
        Baker Co. OMC WW1)
(6) Cherrington, Charles Ira, b. 6/18/1928, d. 12/31/1961

(7) Cherrington, Betty Lou, b. 7/2/1943, d. 7/21/1943
(8) Toulou, Tony Vincent, b. 2/16/1969, d. 3/30/1969

- Gardner Ira's first name is Gardie, on the stone.
- Charles Ira's headstone reads Charlie I.
- Vada and Gardner are on the same stone.

Section 21, Lot 93, Plots 1-8 Lot Owner - Mrs. Will Briggs

(1) Briggs, William Jackson, b. 12/16/1850, d. 8/26/1921
(2) Briggs, Mary Rose Prushafer, b. 7/5/1861, d. 9/14/1936
(3) Briggs, John A., b. 12/4/1900, d. 5/29/1938
(4) Briggs, William Roy, b. 2/14/1898, d. 10/23/1979
(7) Eiker, Letitia Ann Prushafer (Klinck Fun Mk), b. 3/7/1867,
     d. 8/10/1943
(8) Briggs, Ralph Earl, b. 2/15/1921, d. 8/16/1922, (handmade stone)

- William J. and Mary are on the same stone.
- Mary Rose stone reads born 1860, plot record reads 1861.
- John A.'s draft registration card reads born December 6th.

Section 22, Lot 94, Plots 1-8 Lot Owner - Newton Cherrington

(4) Cherrington, Jessie Newton, ILL. Pvt. 39 Inf., b. 10/2/1887,
     d. 7/31/1918
(5) Cherrington, James Andrew, b. 2/1/1892, d. 3/27/1928
(6) Cherrington, John Louis (USA 1917-1919), b. 8/16/1889,
     d. 2/26/1968
(7) Cherrington, Anna A. Norburg w/o Newton, b. 9/14/1865,
     d. 2/21/1949
(8) Cherrington, Newton Ira, b. 2/1/1867, d. 9/4/1934

- Anna and Newton are on the same stone.
- Jessie has two stones, one military.

Section 23, Lot 95, Plots 1-8 Lot Owner - Andrew Norburg

(4) Norburg, Emma, b.?? on plot record, d. 11/24/1918, (NS)
(5) Norburg, August P., b. 11/16/1891, d. 6/21/1970, (NS)
     Obituary shows middle initial as 'E' not 'P'.
(6) Norburg, Joseph, d. 9/9/1917, (NS)
(7) Norburg, Ida Johnson, b. 2/14/1854, d. 4/3/1924 (new stone)
(8) Norburg, Andrew, b. 6/9/1840, d. 3/16/1915

- There is a note in the plot record that says "Andrew's first wife, Betsy Nelson is buried in the H Folund ? Cemetery". The handwriting is not clear. It could be an abbreviation.

Section 24, Lot 96, Plots 1-8 Lot Owner - Nels Nelson

(1) **Nelson**, Nels A ,.b. 4/19/1864, d. 6/27/1912, (NS)

Section 25, Lot 97, Plots 1-8 Lot Owner - Fred Harpman

(1) **Harpman**, Infant Son of F.H. & M.V., b. 1919, d. 1919
(2) **Harpman**, Fred H., b. 6/29/1885, d. abt. 1949
(3) **Harpman**, Melissa Viola Wagher w/o F. H., b. 11/25/1888, d. 6/26/1919
(5) **Goff**, Dolores May, b. 7/16/1931, d. 9/6/1933, (NS)

- Fred and Melissa are on the same stone. There is no death date for Fred, his death year was derived from his obituary.

Section 26, Lot 98, Plots 1-8 Lot Owner - Alfred Myrick

(1) **Myrick**, Hannah Lavern d/o A. & L., b. 1903, d. 1903
(2) **Myrick**, Alfred Leroy, b. 4/3/1866, d. 10/8/1935
(3) **Myrick**, Lucy E. Prushafer w/o A., b. 7/3/1865, d. 10/30/1941
(4) **Myrick**, Lorence D., b. 3/8/1897, d. 5/15/1952
(5) **Myrick**, Guiles L., b. 5/8/1893, d. 12/10/1969
(6) **Myrick**, Brenda Sue, b. 6/27/1958, d. 6/29/1958
(7) **Myrick**, Edna Florence, b. 1/22/1904, d. 7/27/1982

- Alfred and Lucy are on one stone.
- Lorence, Guiles and Brenda are on one stone.
- Edna's headstone reads death date 8/27, the obit. and plot record show 7/27.

Section 27, Lot 99, Plots 1-8 Lot Owner - Walter Dolk

(1) **Dolk**, Ruby Pauline d/o H. W. & M.E., b. 11/16/1918, d. 11/16/1918
(2) **Dolk**, Henry Walter, b. 1890, d. 6/16/1958
(3) **Dolk**, Mary Emma Wagher w/o W., b. 6/11/1896, d. 1/12/1972

- Mary's stone plot record show birth 1897, obit. shows 6/11/1896.

Section 28, Lot 100, Plots 1-8 Lot Owner - Wagher

(1) Wagher, Infant, (NS)
(2) Wagher, John (Jonnie), b. 11/4/1875, d. 6/1/1890
(3) Wagher, Maria M. Moore (Mother), b. 7/12/1837, d. 3/5/1908
(4) Wagher, John H. (Father), b. 4/22/1829, d. 6/6/1896
(5) Wagher, Curtis Phillip, b. 5/18/1858, d. 2/25/1904

- John and Maria are on one stone.

Section 29, Lot 101, Plots 1-4 Lot Owner - Peter Nelson

(2) Nelson, Andrew, b. 1821, d. 1902
(3) Nelson, Anna Peterson, w/o A., b. 1819, d. 1909
(4) Nelson, Peter, b. 1848, d. 5/11/1908

- All three on one stone.

Section 29, Lot 101, Plots 5-8   Lot Owner - Nels Nelson

(6) Nelson, Anna Seaburg, b. 11/26/1862, d. 11/4/1946
(7) Nelson, Nels, b. 1859, d. 1912

- Nels and Anna are both on one stone.

Section 30, Lot 102, Plots 1-8 Lot Owner - Andrew Seaburg

(3) Seaburg, Joseph, b. 8/24/1865, d. 8/11/1948
(4) Seaburg, Emma C., b. 3/1/1868, d. 1/24/1941
(5) Seaburg, Helina (Lina) Sophia Anderson w/o A., b. 9/6/1828,
      d. 9/2/1906
(6) Seaburg, Andrew h/o Helina, b. 8/17/1821, d. 3/13/1908

- Helina and Andrew are on the same stone.
- Plot record shows Andrews death as 3/13, headstone reads 3/18.

Section 31, Lot 103, Plots 1-8 Lot Owner - Gibbs

(1) Gibbs, Robert Russell, b. 8/3/1906, d. 6/27/1918
(2) Gibbs, Willard Howard, b. 7/11/1912, d. 5/18/1929
(7) Gibbs, Abbie May Goff (Mother), b. 6/9/1876, d. 9/25/1957
(8) Gibbs, Robert (Father), b. 12/30/1874, d. 2/13/1951

- There is one large headstone and 4 smaller ones for each individual.

Section 32, Lot 104, Plots 1-4 Lot Owner - Elmer Wagher

(1) Wagher, John Carrol son E.S. & S., b. 1/5/1932, d. 1/8/1932
(2) Wagher, Shella H. Hilton, wife, b. 2/14/1900 d. 1/6/1942
(3) Wagher, Elmer S., b. 2/11/1895, d. 4/22/1959, Pvt. IL. Co. 161
　　Depot Brg. WW1
(4) Wagher, Robert Charles son E.S. & S., b. 4/13/1934, d. 6/11/1950

Section 32, Lot 104, Plots 5-8 Lot Owner - Thomas Wilstead

(7) Wilstead, Charles, b. 4/22/1881, d. 11/17/1881
(8) Wilstead, Infant, b. 10/17/1875, d. 10/17/1875
(9) Wilstead, Bertha, b. 10/16/1876, d. 6/4/1883

- Bertha Wilstead is listed in the plot record and crossed out.

Section 33, Lot 105, Plots 1-8 Lot Owner - Allen Cherrington (no stones)

(1) Cherrington, Rachel Ellen (Ella), b. 10/3/1858, d. 10/1/1926
(2) Henderson,　Sarah Lucretta Cherrington, w/o Homphrey 1st.
　　b. 3/20/1866, d. 6/6/1953
(3) Cherrington, Elizabeth Jane Humphries, b. 12/12/1837,
　　d. 8/18/1910
(4) Cherrington, Allen Wesley, b. 9/24/1832, d. 5/27/1908
(5) Cherrington, Emory S., b. 8/22/1869, d. 12/15/1869
(6) McGrath, Emma Alice Cherrington, b. 4/24/1870,
　　d. 12/13/1946
(7) Cherrington, Getty b. 5/18/1878, d. 11/7/1904
(8) Chambers, Grace Claire Cherrington, b. 5/5/1879, d. 2/2/1955
(9) Cherrington, Lutecia Elizabeth, d. 9/7/1863, Murdered by Jim
　　Botts – Infant.

- Jim Botts went to prison for Lutecia's murder.
- The plot record has Elizabeth's as Humphries, Obit has Humphrey.

Section 34, Lot 106, Plots 1-8 Lot Owner - Wick

(4) Wick, Infant, b. 1911, d. 1911, (NS)

Section 35, Lot 107, Plots 1-4 Lot Owner - Orvil Henry

(1) Henry, Richard, b. 7/24/1938, d. 7/26/1938, (NS)

Section 35, Lot 107, Plots 5-8 Lot Owner - Frank Gibbs

(7) Gibbs, Ruby Jane Buckbee w/o Frank, b. 3/18/1887, d. 7/13/1973
(8) Gibbs, Frank L., b. 12/19/1881, d. 1/23/1952

- The headstone shows Ruby's birth as March 15th. The obit. and plot record read March 18th. Both are on one stone

Section 36, Lot 108, Plots 1-8 Lot Owner - T. J. Gothard

(2) Gothard, Thomas Joseph, b. 1852, d. 1899
(3) Gothard, Sara Patton , b. 12/9/1846, d. 4/23/1918
(4) Gothard, Elizabeth, b. 8/9/1884, d. 10/20/1918
(5) Gothard, Margaret w/o Glenn, b. 2/27/1914, d. 6/30/1992
(6) Gothard, Glenn, b. 12/16/1912, d. 1/25/1983, U.M. Minister
(7) Gothard, Hazel L. Sanquist, b. 2/19/1890, d. 9/1/1980
(8) Gothard, Frank T., b. 10/1/1888, d. 5/23/1969

- Thomas, Sara and Elizabeth are all on the same stone.
- Thomas has another small one for himself
- Frank's middle initial on the plot record is "L", the headstone reads "T"

WESTFALL CEMETERY – NEW ADDITION

The new addition is arranged in a similar manner as the old section except that there are only 4 graves within each Lot. The numbering of the graves within each lot reverses with each new lot going from left to right. For example: facing the front of the Cemetery, Lot 109 is 1,2,3,4 but the lot to the right of it, Lot 120, is 4,3,2,1. This continues all the way across each row. For clarity, those Lots that are reversed have been noted with a **(R)** below. All others, when facing the front of the Cemetery are 1,2,3,4.

Section 1, Lot 109, Lot Owner - Allen Westfall

(2) Martin, Caleb Bronson, b. 5/22/1994, d. 10/30/2001
(3) Westfall, Theresa M. Westfall, b. 8/24/1964, d. 10/13/1980
(4) Westfall, Allen Laverne, b. 12/1/1954, d. 9/7/1975

- Caleb is a new addition, actual plot location is approximated.
- Plot record for Allen has d. 9/10/1975, headstone and obit. has 9/7/1975.

Section 2, Lot 110, Lot Owner - Larry Fitzanko

(1) Fitzanko, Larry K., b. 1940, d. _____
(2) Fitzanko, Charlotte A., b. 1945, d. _____

- Both on one stone. Plot location is best estimate.

Section 3, Lot 111, Plot 1-2 Lot Owner – C. Taylor/M. Gutzmer

- Per a recent family agreement, plots 1 and 2 will now be for Martin and Anne Gutzmer. Chris and Pam Taylor will be in Lot 118 plots 1 and 2.

Section 3, Lot 111, Plot 3-4 Lot Owner – M. Gutzmer/W. Westfall

(4) Westfall, Wendell L. s/o Harry, b. 12/9/1943, d. 11/6/2007

- Per agreement with Martin and Anne Gutzmer, Wendell and Janet Westfall will be in plots 3 and 4.

Section 4, Lot 112, Lot Owner - Harry Westfall

(1) Taylor, Everett (Gene), b. 4/9/1932, d. 6/11/1998
(2) Taylor, Joyce H. Westfall w/o Gene, b. 6/14/1935, d. 5/23/1998
(3) Westfall, Edith Hoffman, b. 5/13/1907, d. 10/9/1991
(4) Westfall, Harry Sr., b. 8/3/1903, d. 8/22/1995

- Joyce and Everett are on one stone.
- Harry and Edith are on one stone.
- The plot record shows Edith and Harry in Lot 117 but this is
  not true. Harry Sr. and Edith are in Lot 112. Lot 112 shows
  Harry Sr. as the owner, Lot 117 shows Harry Jr. as the lot owner.
- Edith's obit. states that she died on October 9th at midnight.
  Her headstone and plot record show her death on October 10th.

Section 5, Lot 113   Lot Owner - Unknown

(1) Unterkircher, Beverly E., b 4/28/1929, d. 7/20/1998
(2) Unterkircher, David D., b. 6/26/1926, d. 3/21/2004

- Beverly and David were married 5/1/1954
- These are new additions, actual plot location is best estimate.

Sections 5 - 6,   Lots 114 - 115 Lot Owners - none

Section 5, Lot 116, Lot Owner Unknown (R)

(3) England, Duane S., b. 12/30/1915, d. 10/24/1998
(4) England, Florence G., b. 6/6/1915, d. 4/2/2008

- Duane and Florence were married 8/19/1939 and they are the
  parents of Nancy, Blanch and Louise, per the headstone.
- These are new additions; actual plot location is best estimate.

Section 4, Lot 117, Lot Owner - Harry Westfall Jr (R)

(4) Westfall, Harry W. Jr., b. 10/23/1941, d. 11/7/2008

Section 3, Lot 118, Lot Owner – W. Westfall/C. Taylor (R)

- Per a recent family agreement, plots 1 and 2 will be for Chris
  and Pam Taylor. Plots 3 and 4 are empty.

Section 2, Lot 119, Lot Owner - Howard Westfall (R)

(1) Westfall, Howard, b. 5/23/1911, d. 7/8/2006
(2) Westfall, Gary, b. 5/20/1938, d. 9/3/1991

- Not sure of actual plot layout for Howard and Gary.

Section 1, Lot 120, Lot Owner - Tom Leazenby (R)

Section 1, Lot 121, Lot Owner - Tom Leazenby

(3) Leazenby, Betty A., b. 7/16/1927, d. _____
(4) Leazenby, Thomas s/o Lenzy E., b. 1/3/1924, d. 8/5/1988

- Both on one stone.
- Thomas also has a stone of his own, Corporal US Army, WWII.

Section 2, Lot 122, Lot Owner - Earl Mitchell

(1) Mitchell, Florence Collison (Mom), b. 7/30/1911, d. 6/1/1980
(2) Mitchell, Sylvanus Earl (Dad), b. 2/15/1903, d. 1/10/1972
(3) Mitchell, Edmund Lee, b. 12/16/1937, d. 9/25/1983, U.S. Army- Korea.

- Florence and Sylvanus are on one stone.
- Edmund is a new addition; actual plot location is best estimate.

Section 3, Lot 123, Lot Owner - none

Section 4, Lot 124, Lot Owner - Shawn Westfall

(4) Taylor, Jerry W., b. 6/14/1956, d. 6/20/2000

- Jerry is the s/o Joyce and Gene, plot location is a best estimate.

Sections 5 - 6, Lot 125 - 128, Lot Owners - none

Section 4, Lot 129, Lot Owner - Rhonda Wilson (R)

(1) Wilson, Rhonda Lee Pine, b. 9/13/1956, d. _____

- This is a new addition; actual plot location is a best estimate.

Section 3, Lot 130, Lot Owner - none listed (R)

Section 2, Lot 131, Lot Owner - Edward Mitchell (R)

Section 1, Lot 132, Lot Owner - William L. Smith (R)

(1) Smith, Teresa Lynn, b. 4/8/1969, d. 4/8/1969

Section 1, Lot 133, Lot Owner - Ed Corum

(1) Corum, Ethel I., b. 7/29/1921, d. 5/27/1981
(2) Corum, Edward A., b. 7/7/1918, d. 3/10/1991

- Both on same stone, actual plot location is a best estimate.

Section 2, Lot 134, Lot Owner - Reed Gibbs

(3) Gibbs, Hazle Payne, b. 11/8/1900, d. 3/23/1990
(4) Gibbs, Reed, b. 1/5/1901, d. 5/31/1972

- Hazle and Reed are both on the same stone.

Sections 4 - 6, Lots 135 - 140, Lot Owners - none

Section 4, Lot 141, Lot Owner - Clarence Marquith (R)

Section 3, Lot 142, Lot Owner - none listed (R)

Section 2, Lot 143, Lot Owner - John England (R)

(2) England, John Albert, b. 4/6/1900, d. 4/16/1967
(3) England, Blanch Helen McBeth, b. 2/19/1898, d. 5/13/1975
(4) Vilardo, Helen E. (England), b. 3/3/1922, d. 6/9/1998

- Blanch is John A.'s wife they are on the same stone.
- Helen's actual plot location is a best estimate.

Section 1, Lot 144, Lot Owner - Charles Cherrington (R)

Section 1, Lot 145, Lot Owner - Charles Cherrington

(1) Pitts, William Lynn, b. 1/24/1941, d. 8/27/1966 USN
(2) Cherrington, Catherine M. Tonkin w/o Pitts and Cherrington,
        b. 12/13/1912, d. 11/7/2006
(3) Cherrington, Charles Alfred, b. 3/2/1907, d. 2/13/2004, (Flag)

Section 2, Lot 146, Lot Owner - Alva England

(3) England, Alva A., b. 3/22/1895, d. 3/13/1967
(4) England, Imo Arlens Saline, wife, b. 8/20/1896, d. 11/28/1996

- Both on one stone.

Section 3, Lot 147, For Sale (Originally marked Harley England)

Section 4, Lot 148, Lot Owner - Clarence Marquith Jr.

(3) Marquith, Beverly "Bev", b. 10/22/1931 d. _____
(4) Marquith, Clarence "Kayo" b. 10/17/1926 d. _____

- Inscription shows married 10/10/1953 and parents of Linda,
JR, Randy & Laura. Both on one stone, location is best estimate.

Section 5 & 6, Lots 149, 150 Lot Owners - none

Section 7, No Lot # 151

Section 8, Lot 152, Lot Owner - McQueen (R)

(1) McQueen, Lloyd L., b. 11/14/1914, d. 9/23/1996
(2) McQueen, Vivian, b. 7/2/1916, d. _____

- New addition, actual location is best estimate.
- One stone for both, inscription reads, "Married 12/17/1938"
and "Parents of Jerald, Joel & Judith.

Section 9, Lot 153, Lot Owner - M. Fields (R)

(1) Fields, John Marshall Jr. s/o J. & G., b. 3/16/1918, d. _____
(2) Fields, Helen Louise Hanson w/o John Jr., b. 9/29/1919, d. _____

- John and Helen are listed in Section 34, Lot 70 also. They are listed here because a headstone is here for them. See note in Section 34, Lot 70.

Section 10, Lot 154, Lot Owner - Neil C. Hurst (R)

(4) Hurst, Neil C., b. 4/26/1924, d. 11/7/1995

- This is a new stone, actual location is best estimate.
- Inscription: Born in Sandusky, Ohio, Loving Father, Faithful Friend.

Section 11, Lot 155, Lot Owner - Charles McDorman (R)

Section 12, Lot 156, Lot Owner - Otho H. Carr (R)

(1) Carr, Otho Harold, b. 3/13/1898, d. 4/4/1966
(2) Carr, Sarah (Sadie) A. Webb w/o Soderquist and Carr,
      b. 1/19/1899, d. 1/16/1983
(3) Carr, Harold L., b. 11/15/1930, d. 12/21/1998
(4) Carr, Norma R., b. 10/23/1921, d. 1/2/1996

- Plot record shows Otho's middle name as Howard but the Obit and headstone read Harold. Otho and Sarah are on the same stone.
- Harold and Norma are on one stone, plot location is a best estimate.

Section 12, Lot 157, Lot Owners - Richard Farrell/Otho H. Carr

(3) Farrell, Dorothy E. Wyman (Mother), b. 12/12/1923, d. 12/6/1967
(4) Farrell, Richard H. (Father), b. 1/30/1913, d. 1/4/1987

Section 11, Lot 158, Lot Owner - Charles Mc Dorman

Section 10, Lot 159, Lot Owner - none listed

(1) Peterson, Madge J., b. 10/19/1918, d. 5/10/1992
(2) Peterson, Everett A., b. 5/3/1913, d. 7/9/1991

- One stone, new addition, plot location is best estimate.

Section 9, Lot 160, Lot Owner - Robert Lemay

(4) Lemay, Jace Allen, b. 4/18/1984, d. 4/18/1984

Section 8, Lot 161 Plot 1-4

(2) **Davis,** Stanley (PFC U.S. Marine Corps), b. 3/9/1931, d. 3/7/1994

Section 7, Lot 162 Plot 1-4

(1) **Oates,** Leroy, b. 11/5/1921, d. _____
(2) **Oates,** Florence (King), b. 2/29/1916, d. 8/7/1995

- One stone, new addition, plot location is best estimate.
- SSN death index shows Leroy Oates died Sept. 11, 2004 in
  Hawthorne, Los Angeles, CA. Birth date matches Nov. 5, 1921

Sections 7 & 9, Lots 163 - 165, Lot Owner - none (R)

Section 10, Lot 166, Lot Owner - Harold Morss (R)

(1) **Palm,** Eugene, b. 10/13/1934, d. 10/7/1998
(2) **Palm,** Janet, b. 10/30/1939, d. _____

- One stone, new addition, plot location is best estimate.

Section 11, Lot 167, Lot Owner - Mrs. Guy Jackson (R)

(2) **Jackson**, Betty, b. 4/9/1928, d. 1/28/1993

Section 12, Lot 168, Lot Owner - Roy Haynes (R)

(3) **Haynes**, Roy B., b. 5/15/1917, d. 4/24/1973, (PFC USA WW2)
(4) **Davis**, Goldie Louise Wyman w/o Haynes and Davis,
      b. 12/30/1925, d. 4/2/1966

Section 12, Lot 169, Lot Owner - Roy Haynes

(2) **Haynes**, Louise Annie, b. 6/19/1954, d. 4/15/1961
(3) **Haynes**, Rickey Lee, b. 6/8/1959, d. 12/15/1959

- Both on one stone.

Section 11, Lot 170, Lot Owners - Forrest Dexter/Richard Smith

Section 10, Lot 171, Lot Owner - none

Section 9, Lot 172, Lot Owner - Richard Carlson

(1) Hymer, Don, Tech 4 US Army WWII Purple Heart, b. 5/7/1920, d. 6/10/1994
(2) Hymer, Katherine B. w/o Don, b. 4/9/1919, d. 12/7/1999

- This is new addition, plot location is best estimate.

Sections 8-12, Lots 173 - 178, Lot Owners - none

Section 11, Lot 179, Lot Owner - Forrest Dexter (R)

Section 12, Lot 180, Lot Owner - unknown (R)

(4) Johnson, John A., b. 2/12/1886, d. 6/18/1966

Section 12, Lot 181, Lot Owner - Arnold Rossell

(1) Rossell, Arnold R., b. 12/30/1932, d. 9/21/2000
(2) Rossell, Carole J., b. 8/9/1935, d. _____

- This is a new addition, plot location is best estimate. Both on one stone. Inscription: Our Sons Michael W. Douglas R., Stephan C., Married 12/1/1957

Section 11, Lot 182, Lot Owner - Forrest Dexter

(1) Dexter, Forrest M., b. 10/6/1923, d. 12/2/2000
(2) Dexter, Evelyn M., b. 1/12/1922, d. _____
(3) Dexter, Thomas L. (Beloved Son & Brother), b. 8/18/1947, d. 7/27/1999
(4) Dexter, Loena F., (Rest in Peace until we meet), b. 9/26/1924, d. 12/27/1949 (Mother)

- Forrest and Evelyn are on one stone.
- All of these are new additions, plot locations are best estimate.

Section 10, Lot 183, Lot Owner - Pat Cherrington

(1) Cherrington, Patrick L., h/o Cathy E., b. 1935, d. _____

(2) Cherrington, Cathy E., w/o Patrick, b. 8/18/1948, d. 9/14/1980

- Both on one stone, married on 1/3/1969.
- This is a new addition, plot locations are estimated.

Sections 9-9, Lots 184 - 188, Lot Owners - none

Section 9, Lot 189 - Lot Owner - none listed (R)

(1) Beckmann, Phyllis V., b. 12/14/1932, d. _____
(2) Beckmann, Ralph D., b. 1/26/1925, d. 12/24/1998
(3) Andrews, Cynthia Jean Beckmann, b. 7/24/1956, d. _____
(4) Andrews, George Charles Jr., b. 5/28/1940, d. 12/19/1998

- Inscription on Phyllis and Ralph's stone "Proud Parents of Cynthia, Patricia and Thomas, married 9/19/1953.
- Ralph has his own stone, EMI US Navy, WWII, Korea,Vietnam.
- Inscription on Cynthia and George's stone, married 9/26/1981.

Section 10, Lot 190, Lot Owner - Richard Resor (R)

(1) Resor, Richard R., b. 5/31/1927, d. 5/21/1991
(2) Resor, Pearl E., b. 1932, d. _____
(4) Peters, Steven E. son ,b. 1955, d. _____

- Pearl and Richard are on one stone, married 5/30/1980
- Richard has his own stone, US Navy WWII.
- All of these are new, plot locations are best estimates.

Section 11, Lot 191, Lot Owner - Forrest Dexter (R)

Section 12, Lot 192, Lot Owner - Charles Murphy (R)

(1) Murphy, Pearl May Briggs, b. 1894, d. 1984, m. 2/26/1914
(2) Murphy, Charles, b. 3/16/1894, d. 2/9/1979

- Both on one stone.

Exceptions-

Those who are listed below were in the original list Compiled by the Knox County Genealogical Society but are not in the actual Plot layout record.

1. **Trick**, Edward F. son S.J. & J.M., d. 5/30/1869, ae 6yr 11m 1d
2. **Monroe**, Ada d/o W.A. & R., d. Aug. 3, 186?, ae 21d
3. **Wyman**, Debra S., d. 4/30/1868, ae 15yr 9m
4. **Arie**, Joseph, b. 6/12/1794, d. 8/26/1869, Joseph is buried in Hope Cemetery per his grand daughter Rhonda.

Part of the Ina White Westfall Collection of those buried in the Cemetery, but not on the plot record.

1. **Crouch**, Josephine S., b. 4/9/1899, d. 8/4/1924

The following graves were identified but the exact Section and Lot could not be determined.

1. **Dawson**, Irvin Murel, b. 1894, d. 8/5/1895
2. **Breasaw**, Charles V., b. 7/18/1926, d. 9/19/1985, located between Gary Westfall and Florence Mitchell, Sect. 2, Lot 119 and Lot 122.
3. **Landrith**, Loren W., b. 10/21/1935, d. 11/29/1990, SP4 U. S
4. **Pickrel**, Nicole Leanne, b. 1/20/1978, d. 7/25/1982
5. **Cherrington**, Thomas, b. 12/28/1939, d. 11/15/2000
6. **Murdock**, Gladys Murphy, b. 6/16/1916, d. 8/11/1988
7. **Murdock**, William L., b. 10/21/1909, d. 1/25/1986
8. **Mahnesmith**, Diana L., b. 5/9/1962, d. 8/10/2001
9. **Mahnesmith**, Clayton E., b. 5/21/1964, d. _____
10. **Westfall**, Robert, b. 2/23/1930, d. 1/20/2000
11. **McDorman**, Charles W. , b. 7/20/1935, d. 4/23/2004
12. **Benge**, Joshua, b. 71/1/1974, d. 2/11/2005
13. **Geraci**, Blanch, b. 1/25/1930, d. 3/30/2003
14. **Gothard**, F. Thomas, b. 1/19/1918, d. 12/11/2005
15. **Gothard**, Jane E., b. 11/16/1917, d. _____, On stone w/F. Thomas
16. **Lingwall**, Donald, b. 10/10/1931, d. 6/27/2003
17. **Lingwall**, Martha, b.6/9/1941, d. 12/14/2006
18. **Swanson**, Esther, b. 11/5/1907, d. 12/19/2005
19. **Westfall**, Marilyn, b. 11/26/1935, d. 10/13/2005, Lot 155
20. **Boynton**, Paula J., b. 6/9/1963, d. 12/16/2006
21. **Unterkircher**, William D., b. 12/15/1954, d. 1/8/2008

22. **Westfall,** Grace Marie, b. 3/8/1902, d. 3/5/1908
23. **Westfall,** Helen Dorothy, b. 7/6/1907, d. 7/7/1907
24. **King,** Roger, b. 8/30/1983, d. 12/2/2004
25. **King,** Kyle b. 6/25/1991, d. 8/28/2007

- Gladys and William Murdock are on the same stone. It is next to Murphy, Sec. 12, Lot 192, Plot 3 & 4. Inscription "and our children, Carol, Billy & Jerry.
- Diana and Clayton are on one stone, married 7/14/1990.

In Circle with Flag Pole

1. **Westergreen,** A. Marion De Voss, b. 11/13/1910, d. 6/26/1993
2. **Westergreen,** Arthur Vincent, b. 7/5/1907, d. 6/11/2004
3. **Seiboldt,** Howard J. Pvt. us Army Air Corps WWII, b .9/24/1916 d. 5/21/1942
4. **Mitchell,** William E. sp3 US Army, Korea, b. 11/27/1930, d. 4/2/1991
5. **Hamerlund,** Rose A., b. 8/10/1931, d. 3/11/2005
6. **Hamerlund,** Carl L., b. 11/6/1929, d. _____
7. **Johnson,** Betty Margarete, b. 10/21/1932, d. 10/1/2001
8. **Johnson,** Gene Max, b. 9/4/1924, d. _____
9. **Williamson,** John W., b. 10/21/1937, d. 5/30/2000
10.**Turner,** Sharon K., b. 11/30/1941, d. 2/23/1994

- A. Marion and Arthur Westergreen are on one large stone in the circle, married 8/17/1947.

INDEX

ABOUT THE AUTHOR

MICHAEL OSLER has been researching his Westfall family line for over twenty years. His own research has been combined with that of a great aunt, Ina White Westfall, whose legacy was to leave him with over forty years of her own research as well. His grandparents, Harry and Edith Westfall; great-grandparents, Frank and Minnie; great-great-grandparents, George and Susan; and great-great-great-grandfather, Alexander are all buried in the Westfall Cemetery along with their descendants. He has successfully traced their roots back to Ohio, West Virginia and New York where the first Westfall came across in the 1600's. The Westfall Cemetery research began eleven years ago when he received the sexton records for the cemetery from his Aunt Joyce Westfall Taylor who is now part of the cemetery as well. It is to her and his great aunt that these books are dedicated.

www.ingramcontent.com/pod-product-compliance
Lightning Source LLC
Chambersburg PA
CBHW070934280326
41934CB00009B/1866